Contents

CW01525143

Map of the units

UNIT	TOPICS	GRAMMAR	VOCABULARY	READING
1 **My community**	New Year celebrations Friends	Present and future tenses State verbs Comparisons	Words with similar meanings Matching expressions with similar meanings	Part 5: multiple-choice questions
2 **Home and away**	Adventure and travel Where you live	Adverb formation Past tenses	Word building (1): adjective suffixes (-ed, -ing) Cities, towns and villages	Part 6: gapped text
3 **Performance**	Music Film and theatre	Linking words The passive	Music Film and cinema	Part 7: multiple matching
4 **Fit and healthy**	Sport Health	Modal verbs Prepositions: at, in, on	Sport Food Word building (2): noun suffixes (-ence, -ity, -(s/t)ion)	Part 5: multiple-choice questions
5 **Lessons learnt**	Achievements Education	Conditionals	Phrasal verbs Careers Education	Part 7: multiple matching
6 **Our planet**	Environment Wildlife	Countable and uncountable nouns Articles so and such (a/an), too and enough	Climate Environmental problems Animals	Part 6: gapped text
7 **Influences**	Buying and selling People and feelings	Verbs and expressions followed by to + infinitive or -ing form Reported speech	Shopping Feelings	Part 5: multiple-choice questions
8 **Breakthrough**	Technology Science	Relative clauses	Technology Science Word building (3): prefixes and suffixes	Part 7: multiple matching

Official Cambridge Exam Preparation

COMPACT

FIRST
FOR SCHOOLS
THIRD EDITION

B2

TEACHER'S BOOK
WITH DIGITAL PACK

Jessica Smith

Shaftesbury Road, Cambridge CB2 8EA, United Kingdom

One Liberty Plaza, 20th Floor, New York, NY 10006, USA

477 Williamstown Road, Port Melbourne, VIC 3207, Australia

314–321, 3rd Floor, Plot 3, Splendor Forum, Jasola District Centre, New Delhi – 110025, India

103 Penang Road, #05–06/07, Visioncrest Commercial, Singapore 238467

Cambridge University Press & Assessment is a department of the University of Cambridge.

We share the University's mission to contribute to society through the pursuit of education, learning and research at the highest international levels of excellence.

www.cambridge.org
Information on this title: www.cambridge.org/9781009167185

© Cambridge University Press & Assessment 2013, 2014, 2023

First published 2013
Second edition 2014
Third edition 2023

20 19 18 17 16 15 14 13 12 11 10 9 8 7 6 5 4 3 2 1

Printed in Great Britain by Ashford Colour Press Ltd.

A catalogue record for this publication is available from the British Library

ISBN 978-1-009-16718-5 Teacher's Book

Additional resources for this publication at www.cambridge.org/compact

USE OF ENGLISH	WRITING	LISTENING	SPEAKING
Part 1: multiple-choice cloze	Part 1: Essay understanding the question, paragraphing, linking words and phrases	Part 3: multiple matching	Part 1: leisure activities Part 2: comparing ways of spending free time
Part 2: open cloze Part 3: word formation	Part 2: Story sequencing, using a range of past tenses, adjectives and adverbs	Part 1: multiple-choice questions with short recordings	Part 3: discussing preferences, agreeing and disagreeing Part 4: talking about where you live
Part 4: key-word transformations	Part 2: Review organising paragraphs, recommending, using linking words and phrases	Part 4: multiple-choice questions with long recording	Part 1: adding extra information and comments Part 2: talking about films and music, avoiding unknown words, giving preferences
Part 2: open cloze Part 3: word formation	Part 2: Email and letter giving advice, making suggestions, persuading, beginnings and endings	Part 2: sentence completion	Part 3: asking for and reacting to opinions Part 4: discussing sports and keeping fit
Part 1: multiple-choice cloze Part 4: key-word transformations	Part 2: Article keeping the reader's attention, describing and linking	Part 2: sentence completion	Part 1: discussing ambitions, achievements and education Part 2: making guesses
Part 2: open cloze	Part 2: Review understanding the question, recommending	Part 4: multiple-choice questions with long recording	Part 3: agreeing, disagreeing, making a comment or suggestion Part 4: discussing ways of helping the environment
Part 4: key-word transformations	Part 2: Email and letter giving information, using linking words and phrases	Part 3: multiple matching	Part 1: expressing likes and dislikes Part 2: comparing different ways of shopping
Part 3: word formation	Part 1: Essay using a range of vocabulary	Part 1: multiple-choice questions with short recordings	Part 3: structuring a conversation Part 4: discussing technology

Compact Components

WORKBOOK WITHOUT ANSWERS WITH EBOOK

Each unit has four pages of activities providing further practice and consolidation of the language and exam skills presented in the Student's Book. Students can access and download audio files and grammar animations using the QR codes. The Workbook also provides access to the interactive **eBook** and audio via the code on the inside front cover.

STUDENT'S DIGITAL PACK

LEARN MORE ABOUT YOUR COMPACT DIGITAL PACK

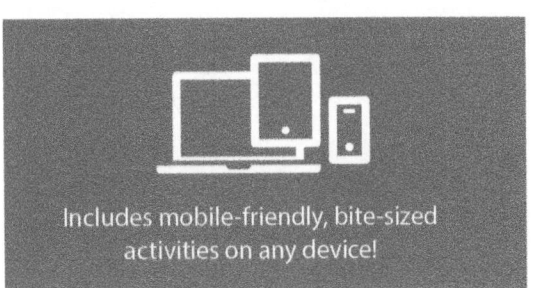

Includes mobile-friendly, bite-sized activities on any device!

TEACHER'S BOOK WITH DIGITAL PACK

The Teacher's Book includes step-by-step activities for each stage of the lesson, with answer keys, background information, extra activities and photocopiable Workbook audioscripts. The Teacher's Book also provides access to the **Digital Pack** via the code on the inside front cover.

TEST GENERATORS

The Test Generators allow you to build your own tests for each unit, term and end-of-year assessment. Tests are available at two levels: Standard and Plus. Speak to your Cambridge representative for details.

PRESENTATION PLUS

Presentation Plus is easy-to-use, interactive classroom presentation software that helps you deliver effective and engaging lessons. It includes the Student's Book and Workbook content and allows you to present and annotate content and link to the online resources. Speak to your Cambridge representative for details.

B2 First for Schools exam information

Part/Timing	Content	Exam focus
Reading and Use of English 1 hour 15 minutes	**Part 1** A modified cloze text containing eight gaps and followed by eight multiple-choice items. **Part 2** A modified open cloze text containing eight gaps. **Part 3** A text containing eight gaps. Each gap corresponds to a word. The stems of the missing words are given beside the text and must be changed to form the missing word. **Part 4** Six separate questions, each with a lead-in sentence and a gapped second sentence to be completed in two to five words, one of which is given as a 'key word'. **Part 5** A text followed by six multiple-choice questions. **Part 6** A text from which six sentences have been removed and placed in a jumbled order after the text. A seventh sentence, which does not need to be used, is also included. **Part 7** A text, or several short texts, preceded by ten multiple-matching questions.	Candidates are expected to demonstrate the ability to apply their knowledge of the language system by completing the first four tasks; candidates are also expected to show understanding of specific information, text organisation features, tone, and text structure.
Writing 1 hour 20 minutes	**Part 1** One compulsory essay question presented through a rubric and short notes. **Part 2** Candidates choose one task from a choice of three task types. The tasks are situationally based and presented through a rubric and possibly a short input text. The task types are: • an essay • an article • an email or letter • a review • a report	Candidates are expected to be able to write using different degrees of formality and different functions: advising, comparing, describing, explaining, expressing opinions, justifying, persuading, recommending and suggesting.
Listening Approximately 40 minutes	**Part 1** A series of eight short unrelated extracts from monologues or exchanges between interacting speakers. There is one three-option multiple-choice question per extract. **Part 2** A short talk or lecture on a topic, with a sentence-completion task which has ten items. **Part 3** Five short related monologues, with five multiple-matching questions. **Part 4** An interview or conversation, with seven multiple-choice questions.	Candidates are expected to be able to show understanding of agreement, attitude, detail, function, genre, gist, main idea, opinion, place, purpose, relationship, situation, specific information, topic, etc.
Speaking 14 minutes	**Part 1** A conversation between the examiner (the 'interlocutor') and each candidate (spoken questions). **Part 2** An individual 'long turn' for each candidate, with a brief response from the second candidate (visual and written stimuli, with spoken instructions). **Part 3** A discussion question with five written prompts. **Part 4** A discussion on topics related to Part 3 (spoken questions).	Candidates are expected to be able to respond to questions and to interact in conversational English.

1 My community

UNIT OBJECTIVES

TOPICS: New Year celebrations, family and friends, daily life

GRAMMAR: present and future tenses, comparisons

VOCABULARY: words with similar meanings

READING AND USE OF ENGLISH PART 1: using context to choose answers

PART 5: understanding the task

WRITING PART 1: writing an essay

LISTENING PART 3: listening for details and general understanding

SPEAKING PART 1: giving extended answers

PART 2: making comparisons between two photos, answering the question

Listening

STARTER

With books closed, introduce the topic by writing the word *Celebration* on the board and asking students to brainstorm vocabulary they associate with the word. Encourage them to think about events and dates they celebrate and what they do when they celebrate. Make a note of any useful or new words on the board for students to use when they answer the questions in the Student's Book.

1 Focus attention on the photos and elicit answers to the questions from around the class. Encourage students to justify their answers and say whether they agree or disagree with their classmates' answers.

2 Tell the class to answer the questions in pairs. Move round the class and provide help with vocabulary if needed. Elicit feedback from a few different pairs.

Part 3

3 🔊 **02** Read through the questions with the class, checking understanding before asking students to listen to the recording to identify the answers.

> **Answers**
> 1 family (including aunts, uncles, cousins)
> 2 her family
> 3 no (it was the most memorable ever because of the sharing of stories)

> **Audio script Track 02**
>
> Anita: I celebrated last New Year's Eve in Mumbai at home with loads of my family, including aunts, uncles and cousins. The first part of the evening went as expected – games followed by dancing to Bollywood songs – but about half an hour before midnight, we'd all had enough. But then my eldest cousin suggested taking it in turns to talk about our year. We all learnt so much about each other from sharing our thoughts on the year just gone – it made us feel even closer as a family. So thanks to my cousin, it became the most memorable New Year's Eve ever!

4 🔊 **02** Check whether students are familiar with the format of Listening Part 3. If necessary, ask questions to elicit details. For example, *How many recordings do you hear in the exam?* (five), *How many people are speaking in each recording?* (one), *What do they have in common?* (They are all talking about the same topic), *How many questions are there?* (five, one for each speaker, with eight answer options to choose from), *How many times do you hear the recording?* (twice).

Go over the exam tips with the class and point out that it is important that students listen for detailed understanding rather than just individual words, which may be used as distraction. It's important to check carefully for the meaning of whole phrases and match them with the question rather than just focusing on single words. Remind them that they will hear the recording twice.

Play the recording again and encourage students to discuss their answers with a partner. Check answers as a class, eliciting explanations for the answer selected.

> **Answer**
> C

✓ Exam task

Give students time to read the instructions. Point out that students can eliminate answer option C as they have already used it for Anita in Ex 4.

🔊 **03** Play the recording of the two speakers twice and make sure students have checked their answers before going through them with the class.

> **Exam task answers**
> Speaker 1 A
> Speaker 2 B

Audio script Track 03

You will hear two people talking about how they celebrated New Year. Choose from the list A–D what each speaker says about how they celebrated it.

Speaker 1: In February, I celebrated Chinese New Year at my grandparents' home in Hong Kong with family. We'd spent several days before it busily preparing, and I felt just as much excitement as when I was a little kid. Grandad had cleaned the house from top to bottom, hung red decorations on the walls, and filled the kitchen with delicious dishes. As we sat down to eat, everyone dressed in red, I suddenly felt a strong curiosity about why we did all these things. So over dinner, I got Grandma to explain what they meant. She's great at telling stories, so we all sat listening to her happily while we were eating.

Speaker 2: Most people here in Bilbao, Spain spend New Year's Eve at home with their families and let off fireworks at midnight to signal the New Year beginning. The last one was special for my family because in September, my sister's going to live in New Zealand for two years. It was a really emotional evening, knowing that when she's gone, we'll have to spend this time of year without her. She did her best to cheer us up, and we had a lovely dinner. Then at midnight we watched the celebrations in Madrid on TV and ate 12 grapes as usual, a custom that's supposed to bring us good luck for the coming year.

FURTHER PRACTICE

Put students into small groups to tell each other about the most recent or the best celebration they have had with family or friends, and tell the other members of the group to ask questions to elicit as much detail as they can.

Reading and Use of English

Part 1

Vocabulary – Words with similar meanings

STARTER

Elicit anything students know or remember about Reading and Use of English Part 1. Ask what the task looks like and what they have to do. Students look at the exam task in the book to check their ideas. Point out that in order to select the correct answer, students need to identify the differences between words with similar meanings.

1 Direct students' attention to the instructions and give pairs two or three minutes to complete the task, then check answers together.

> **Answers**
> 1 distinguish   2 highlight   3 enhance   4 expose
> 5 distinguish

2 Read through the instructions with the class. Point out that students need to use the underlined words to decide which answer is correct. This exercise is checking whether students can identify which preposition follows each verb. In the exam task the words are not underlined but students should learn to look for and identify these clues. Allow a few minutes to read the sentences and choose the correct answer before checking answers as a class.

> **Answers**
> 1 consisted   2 involved   3 contributed   4 participated

FURTHER PRACTICE

Students can work in pairs to make their own sentences using some of the words in Ex 1 and 2.

3 Draw attention to the photo and the title of the text and elicit suggestions as to what International Youth Day is. Set a time limit of one or two minutes to encourage students to read the text quickly to find the answers to the questions. Students can check their answers with a partner before class feedback. Point out that in the exam students should read through the text quickly to get a general idea of what it is about before focusing on the gaps.

> **Answers**
> 1   12th August every year
> 2   conferences, concerts, sporting events, parades and mobile exhibitions

✅ Exam task

Read through the instructions with the class, reminding them to think about the differences in meaning in the four answer options and to carefully read the words before and after each gap in the text before making their choice. Read through the exam tip with the class and remind students of the grammar they practised in Ex 2 (dependent prepositions). They should also look at the grammatical forms which may follow the word in the gap, such as typical linking words like *despite* or *although*. Go over the example with the class, eliciting why the other words do not fit the gap (incorrect meaning). Allow students ten minutes to complete the task.

4 Explain how important it is for students to check their answers when they finish. This is especially important in an exam when they might be nervous. Go over the answers with the class, encouraging students to explain why they eliminated the incorrect answer options each time.

> **Exam task answers**
> 1 D   2 A   3 C   4 B   5 B   6 D   7 C   8 C

Speaking

Part 1

STARTER

Before focusing attention on the task, elicit anything students know or remember about Speaking Part 1. If necessary, ask questions such as *How long is this part?* (two minutes), *Who do you speak to?* (the examiner), *What types of topics might be covered in the questions?* (school, leisure time, future plans, etc.).

1 🔊 **04** Draw attention to the exam tip and explain that they will hear two candidates giving extended answers to the questions in the box. After students have read the questions, play the recording and ask them to make notes under the Extra information heading as they listen. Students compare their notes with a partner before listening to the recording again if necessary.

> **Answers**
> 1 every Wednesday after school, favourite time
> 2 relax first and play video games
> 3 (Saturdays) friends at the cinema, watching movies, eating popcorn; (Sunday mornings) grandmother
> 4 (Saturday) cycle to town to meet friends as usual, probably go shopping; (Sunday) practise piano for concert on Thursday

2 🔊 **04** Allow a few minutes for students to read the extracts from the recording and complete the gaps from memory. Repeat the recording before checking answers as a class.

> **Answers**
> 1 'm learning   2 get; play   3 'm going to cycle
> 4 'll probably go   5 'll be practising   6 'm playing

> **Audio script Track 04**
>
> Examiner: First, we'd like to know something about you. Do you do any activities after school, Luca?
>
> Luca: Yes, I do. I'm learning to play tennis, so I have a lesson every Wednesday after school on the tennis court. That's my favourite time in the whole week.
>
> Examiner: When do you do your homework?
>
> Luca: When I get home from school, I play video games. I like to relax for an hour, so I prefer to do my homework after dinner.
>
> Examiner: Julie, what do you usually do at the weekend?
>
> Julie: I usually meet my friends at the cinema on Saturdays and we spend all afternoon watching movies and eating popcorn. On Sunday mornings I go to see my grandmother.
>
> Examiner: What are you going to do next weekend?
>
> Julie: On Saturday I'm going to cycle to town to meet my friends as usual, but we'll probably go shopping. And on Sunday I'll be practising my piano most of the day as I'm playing in a concert next Thursday. I know I need to practise a lot before that!

✓ Exam task

Point out to students that the exam is an opportunity to demonstrate to the examiner how much they know. They will get a better result if they use a variety of structures and words. Remind students to use their own ideas to answer the questions and extend their answers with extra detail. Encourage students to listen carefully to their partner's answers and think about whether they gave extended answers with reasons or examples and not just one- or two-word responses. Ask one or two students to report their partner's answers to the class and highlight any good vocabulary or structures they used. Refer students to the Speaking bank on page 108 for further information if needed.

> **FURTHER PRACTICE**
> Ask students to think of two or three more questions about habits and plans. They then take turns asking and answering those questions with their partner.

Part 2

STARTER
Ask the class what they know or remember about Speaking Part 2. Try to elicit the key points by asking questions, if necessary. For example, *What do you have to talk about?* (two photos), *How long do you have to speak for?* (one minute), *What do you have to say about the photos?* (compare them and answer the question at the top of the page), *What happens when you finish your turn?* (your partner is asked a question about your photos and can speak for up to 30 seconds).

3 Draw attention to the photos and put students into pairs to do the task. Elicit answers from around the class and allow students to add any other appropriate words or expressions they know.

> **Answers**
> a quiet spot, concentrate, countryside, energetic, excited, exercise, fresh air, in the distance, in the shade, indoors, outdoors, relax

4 🔊 **05** Explain that this is an example of the type of question students may have to answer about the photos. Point out that generating ideas is an important part of being able to answer the question appropriately in the exam. Younger students often need practice in thinking what to say in this part of the exam as well as how to say it. Allow two or three minutes for students to make notes of some advantages of each situation and then play the recording to listen to Julie's answers. Ask if anyone listed the same ideas as Julie. Remind students that all advantages they think of are valid and there is not only one correct answer.

> **Answers**
> Photo A: they're in the fresh air, having fun together
> Photo B: getting more exercise, more energetic

> **Audio script Track 05**
>
> Julie: In both of the photographs the people are exercising but I think the people in the first photograph are probably much happier than the boy in the second one. They're walking in the countryside, whereas the person in the second photo is inside doing a workout at home, which isn't as enjoyable as being in the fresh air. Also, this person is doing things on his own instead of having fun together. On the other hand, he is probably getting more exercise as he is being more energetic than the people in the first photograph. In the first photograph there is a group of friends or maybe classmates and they're excited about going somewhere together. They're probably chatting as well. They'll spend more time walking than doing an online workout.

☑ Exam task

Read through the exam tip with the class to remind them they have to answer the question and compare the photos within one minute. Go over the instructions and explain that one student in each pair will play the 'examiner' and one the 'candidate' so that they each have a turn to talk about the photos. The 'examiner' should keep an eye on the time rather than the 'candidate'. In the exam, students will not be able to look at a clock so it is helpful to get to know what it feels like to speak for one minute. When they have finished, the listening partner has to speak for up to 30 seconds when answering the follow-up question. Remind students that if they can't remember a word, they should continue speaking by paraphrasing if possible. It's important for them to be able to continue speaking without too much hesitation even if they don't know or remember a specific word. Monitor the class as they do the task. When everyone has finished, elicit some feedback about how they and their partner performed, and address any particular difficulties they had.

Refer students to the Speaking bank on page 110 for further information if needed.

Grammar

Present and future tenses

Students can use the QR code(s) to access *Grammar on the Move*, a short, animated video with explanations and examples of the grammar focus of this unit. If you wish, you can ask students to watch the video before the lesson, or it could be used as a follow up for reinforcement or extra practice. Students do not need to have seen the video in order to do the tasks in the book.

1 Encourage pairs to reread the sentences in Ex 2 on page 8 before working together to answer the questions. Go through the answers with the class, eliciting more example sentences for each tense/use. Refer students to the Grammar reference on page 81 as necessary.

> **Answers**
> 1   present continuous ('m learning)
> 2   present simple (get home, play video games)
> 3   intention ('m going to cycle); *will* – uncertain future plan ('ll probably go)
> 4   future continuous as it's over a period of time ('ll be practising)
> 5   present continuous – definite plan ('m playing)

2 Allow students a few minutes to read the sentences and then elicit the answer and explanation.

> **Answer**
> A is correct in each case as they are all state verbs which cannot be used in continuous tenses.

3 It may be necessary to remind students or explain that some of these verbs can be used in the continuous form when they are used with a different meaning. For example, *think* when expressing an opinion is different to *think* when describing mental activity (compare: *I think that film is great!* and *I'm thinking about my homework*). Also *have* in expressions such as *have breakfast, have a shower*.

Students work individually to choose the correct answers before checking their answers with a partner. This is a general review of present and future verb forms so students need to think about state verbs but also about the appropriate tense in each sentence. Go over the answers with the class, eliciting explanations of why students chose each answer. Refer students to the Grammar reference on page 81 to review rules as needed.

> **Answers**
> 1 want   2 usually stay   3 're meeting   4 're going
> 5 think   6 arrive   7 'm having   8 leave
> 9 'm writing; 'm going to arrive   10 're going

Comparisons

Before or after the lesson refer students to the QR code to access *Grammar on the Move*.

4 Elicit or explain how to make the comparative form of shorter and longer adjectives (adjective + *er* / *more* + adjective + *than*). Then try to elicit other structures used to make comparisons. For example (*not*) *as* + adjective + *as*, *less* + adjective + *than* or *more/less* + noun + *than*. Students should look at the photos as they put the words in the correct order in each sentence. Allow time for students to compare their answers with a partner before class feedback. Refer students to the Grammar reference on page 82 as necessary.

> **Answers**
> 1   are probably much happier than
> 2   will spend more time walking than
> 3   isn't as enjoyable as being
> 4   are probably getting more exercise
> 5   is being more energetic than

5 Refer students to the photos and encourage them to use a range of comparative structures and the words in the box to write sentences about them. Students read their sentences to a partner before class feedback.

> **Suggested answers**
> Playing video games is much less fun than playing miniature golf with friends.
> Playing video games can be far more expensive than miniature golf, at first.
> Playing miniature golf isn't as thrilling as playing an exciting video game.

Reading and Use of English

Vocabulary – Matching expressions with similar meanings

1 Read the instructions with the class, explaining that when the reading comprehension questions have multiple-choice answer options, students need to be able to find words in the text which have similar meanings to those in the options. Students work individually to complete the task before checking their answers with a partner. Go over the answers with the class.

> **Answers**
> 1 insecure   2 a consequence of   3 nature   4 characters
> 5 circle   6 find yourself   7 anxiety

Part 5

2 Draw attention to the photo and encourage students to speculate about the people they can see. Remind them to use modal verbs such as *may, might* and *could*. Tell students that they should try to use a range of structures when they are speaking as this will help them get a better result in the Speaking test. Elicit some suggestions from around the class.

> **Suggested answers**
> 1   friends – similar age, having fun
> 2   having fun, posing for a photo, taking a photo, walking outside
> 3   may post it on a social networking site, e.g. Instagram, Facebook, to show friends and family what they are doing (and possibly what a great, fun life they have / how popular they are!)

3 Go over the exam tip, explaining that the title helps to focus on the topic of the text before they start reading. Then read the questions with the class and set a time limit of two minutes to encourage them to read the text quickly and find the answers without trying to understand every word. Check answers as a class.

> **Answers**
> 1   B how the writer and others feel about their friendships
> 2   two classmates, Lyla and Jonathan

✓ Exam task

Ask the class what they know or remember about Reading and Use of English Part 5. Read through the instructions and questions with the class, pointing out that this task is different from the task in the live exam in two ways. It is shorter and there is some extra information about the questions to help guide students through the different types of question they may find. Explain that the incorrect answers in this part of the exam are often 'distractors' which are designed to tempt candidates into giving the wrong answer, so they should try to eliminate incorrect answers as well as selecting the correct ones. With a less confident class you may choose to read each explanation and subsequent question as a group and work through the questions, gradually checking understanding as you go. Alternatively, you could check understanding and then allow students time to look for the answers individually before checking them as a class.

> **Exam task answers**
> 1 C   2 C   3 D   4 D

> **FURTHER PRACTICE**
> Using the ideas and some of the vocabulary in the text, students talk to a partner about which person in the text they are most similar to, and why.

Writing

Part 1 essay

1 2 3 Read through questions 1, 2 and 3 with the class, dealing with any queries, and then put students into pairs to ask and answer the questions. Encourage students to extend their answers, saying why and giving examples in question 3. Monitor and provide support as needed. Elicit some answers from around the class and make a note of any useful or new vocabulary on the board so that students can use it in their essays.

4 Ask students if they know or remember anything about Writing Part 1. Ask one or two questions to elicit general information. For example, *What is the difference between Part 1 and Part 2?* (Part 1 is compulsory and in Part 2 there is a choice of questions), *What type of text do you have to write?* (an essay). Then ask students to read the true/false questions in pairs before looking for the answers in the exam task opposite. Go over the task with the class, encouraging students to justify their answers. Point out that the format for Writing Part 1 is always the same with a question to answer, two points to include and another point to add. Before asking students to read the model answer, elicit suggestions for the 'your own idea' prompt from around the class.

Answers
1 F (You have no choice. There is one essay task and you have to do it. It's compulsory.)
2 F (You have to write between 140 and 190 words. 190 is the maximum.)
3 T (It gives you the topic.)
4 T (family and friends)
5 T (Yes, you are asked to give a general opinion, although you can give examples from your own life and experience as well.)
6 T (Yes, it should be a fresh idea.)

5 Direct students' attention to the model answer and ask them to read it through quickly to identify whether the writer thinks friends or family are more important to young people. (friends). Then put students into pairs to complete the table. Discuss whether the style of the essay is formal or informal and ask students to identify examples to support their ideas. (Formal style is indicated by the use of the linking expressions, the lack of contractions, and some of the vocabulary such as *rely heavily*, *share the same tastes*.)

Answers
2 family
3 teenagers get on better with friends
Conclusion: friends are more important than family
The essay is written in a formal style.

6 Explain that the expressions in the box are useful in an essay or any other piece of formal writing in order to help organise the text and allow the reader to follow the ideas more easily. In the exam students should try to use a range of different linking words and expressions. Ask students to find and underline the expressions in the essay and read the words around them to understand how they are used.

Answers
By the time they are about 14, young people probably spend more time with their friends than with their family. They are at school every day and <u>therefore</u> in the company of their friends. <u>In addition</u>, they play sport with these friends, go into town with them or go round to their houses at the weekend.
<u>Yet</u> all young people still rely heavily on their families, and their parents especially, for support and advice. Parents have more experience and more knowledge to share than friends, and can help with important decisions. For many people family are always part of their life. <u>In contrast</u>, some friendships can get forgotten as people get older.
<u>In general</u> though, I would say that most young people get on better with their friends than their families. They are the same age; <u>for that reason</u> they often share the same tastes in music and clothes and so on. <u>As for</u> ideas, those are often similar too. <u>As a result</u>, parents are often much less important to their children at this stage.
<u>Overall</u>, I personally think that for most teenagers, their friends are more important than their family.

7 Deal with any queries about use or meaning before asking students to read the text and choose the correct linking expression in each case.

Answers
1 in general   2 As for   3 In fact   4 For that reason
5 Yet   6 In contrast

8 Read the exam tips with the class. Students may need support in making a plan. Point out that they should not write long sentences but just make notes of their ideas and brainstorm some useful vocabulary as well as thinking about what idea to include for point 3. It is a good idea to separate the notes into paragraphs before starting to write. Encourage students to show their plan to a partner and explain their ideas.

✅ Exam task

Set a time limit of about 30 minutes for students to write and then check their essay. In the exam students will have 40 minutes to plan, write and check their work.

Refer students to the Writing bank on page 96 for further information if needed.

Model answer
Leaving home to go to university when you are young can be a very exciting time. However, it may be the first time you have lived away from your parents, so it can also be stressful. When you live with parents, you are given support in many ways. They help you emotionally, financially and with practical things like cooking meals or giving you lifts. It is hard to learn to live without such support, so continuing to live at home is easier. Your parents carry on taking care of you, and you are able to concentrate on your studies.
On the other hand, if you live in student accommodation with friends, you have far more freedom to do what you want. You don't have to live by your parents' rules. Learning to manage your money and keep a home are essential life lessons, which you can learn better if you are living independently. Furthermore, if you live in accommodation with other students, it is easier to make friends. The young people you live with are all facing the same challenges as you, which may lead to the development of strong friendships that can last a lifetime.
In conclusion, there are benefits and disadvantages to living away from the family. But learning to be independent is an important life skill.

2 Home and away

UNIT OBJECTIVES

TOPICS: adventure and travel, where you live

GRAMMAR: adverb formation, past tenses

VOCABULARY: word building, cities, towns and villages

READING AND USE OF ENGLISH PART 6: using nouns and pronouns to understand cohesion

PART 2: understanding the task

PART 3: adjective suffixes

WRITING PART 2: writing a story

LISTENING PART 1: listening for detail

SPEAKING PART 3: agreeing and disagreeing

PART 4: expressing and justifying opinions

Reading and Use of English

STARTER
Introduce the topic of the unit by asking the class to suggest the names of some activities that they would classify under the heading of *Adventures*. Note any new vocabulary on the board.

1 Elicit the names of the activities in the photos (polar trekking, base jumping, rock/free climbing) before putting students into pairs to answer the questions. After a few minutes, elicit some answers from around the class to compare ideas.

> **Answers**
> A polar trekking
> B base jumping
> C rock climbing

Part 6

2 Draw attention to the text and the title and ask students to read and find the answer to the question. Set a time limit of one minute to encourage them to scan the text for the answer without trying to understand every word at this stage.

> **Answer**
> They do a long training programme and then go on a trip to Iceland followed by a ten-day trek across Greenland.

3 Focus students' attention on the exam task (on page 15) and give them a few minutes to read the instructions. Then ask for suggestions on how best to approach this type of task. If possible, elicit that it is a good idea to

read the title and then the whole text quickly to get an idea of the topic. Then, students should look at sentences A–G. Finally, they should read the words around the gaps in the text to find links such as verb tenses, pronouns and linking expressions. Tell students that before they do the exam task they are going to work through some preparation exercises to practise these steps.

Read the exam tip with the class and tell them that this exercise gives them a chance to practise the skill described. If necessary, go through the first question with the class, asking *Who is the explorer?* to check understanding and then allow students time to complete the exercise individually. Check answers as a class.

> **Answers**
> 1 Gemma Mann
> 2 The Nordic Exploration Club
> 3 students who are selected for the trek
> 4 the trip to Iceland and trek across Greenland
> 5 the training and the trek
> 6 those who have done the trek

4 Point out that this exercise asks students to use the same skill as in Ex 3 as they identify the nouns that the pronouns refer to. Students can work in pairs or individually before checking answers as a class.

> **Answers**
> 1 many teenagers had very little self-confidence and lacked motivation
> 2 the major trek across the Arctic
> 3 Greenland
> 4 other people
> 5 the participants'

✓ Exam task

Remind students of the importance of reading the instructions carefully as well as looking at the picture and the title as these provide the context for the reading text. Set a time limit of around 15 minutes for students to complete the task. Don't go over the answers until students have completed Ex 5.

5 In pairs, students discuss their answers and justify their choices by explaining which words and phrases the answer options connect to in the text. Go over the answers to the exam task as a class, eliciting this information at the same time.

> **Exam task answers**
> 1 F   2 C   3 A   4 E   5 G   6 B

Speaking

Part 3

1 Students work on their own to answer the questions before telling a partner their answers.

2 Check understanding of the phrases in the box by eliciting sentences from different students around the class about their personal preferences. Then put students into groups to compare opinions.

3 Lead a brief class discussion to answer the questions.

4 Students do the task on their own and then check answers with a partner before class feedback.

> **Answers**
> A I agree with you. That's what I think too. I think you're right.
> D I think it would be better to … I disagree.

✓ Exam task

Ask the class what they know or remember about Speaking Part 3. If necessary, use questions to elicit details. For example, *How many phases (parts) are there?* (two), *Who do you speak to?* (your partner), *What do you have to talk about in each phase?* (the question written in the centre of the page in phase 1 and then a summing-up type question in phase 2), *How long should you speak for?* (two minutes in phase 1 and one minute in phase 2), *Do you have to discuss all the ideas on the page?* (No, but you should aim for a minimum of three), *Do you have to agree with your partner?* (no).

Read through the instructions and look at the question with the class, clearing up any doubts they may have. Point out that the Speaking test is usually done with a partner, but at the end of an exam session, if there is an odd number of candidates there will be a group of three so they should practise doing Speaking Part 3 with one and two partners. If there is a group of three, the time is extended from two to three minutes in phase 1 and from one to two minutes in phase 2 to allow each candidate the same opportunity to speak. They will have about 15 seconds to read the question before starting.

It is important for students to understand that the examiner manages the timing of the two phases and they should not attempt to answer the phase 2 question (*Now decide which two places should be built*) during phase 1.

Before starting the task remind students that they should listen to their partners' ideas and then agree or disagree with them, giving reasons, before moving on to talk about another place. Time the interaction so that students start to get an idea of how long they have to speak for. After three minutes, interrupt the discussions and allow another two minutes for students to answer the phase 2 question.

Hold a brief feedback session to comment on any aspects of performance you noticed while monitoring, and to give students the chance to ask any remaining questions about the task.

Refer students to the Speaking bank on page 114 for further information if needed.

Part 4

Elicit anything students know or remember about Speaking Part 4. If necessary, explain that the examiner asks each candidate to express their opinion on topics related to the discussion in Part 3. Sometimes candidates may be asked to discuss their ideas with their partner and other times they may be asked to comment on their partner's ideas. Part 4 lasts for four minutes, so each candidate will be asked approximately three or four questions.

5 Allow students time to read through the words and phrases in the box and select those that can be used to describe where they live. Help with any unknown vocabulary or pronunciation as necessary.

6 Go over the examples with the class before putting students into pairs to answer the questions. Elicit some answers from around the class.

✓ Exam task

Read the exam tip with the class before putting students into pairs to ask and answer the questions. Encourage them to agree or disagree with their partner, giving reasons. Elicit some feedback from students on their partner's performance by asking questions such as *Did they extend their answers with reasons and examples? Did they use some of the expressions to agree or disagree with your ideas? Did they give examples to support their ideas or opinions?*

Refer students to the Speaking bank on page 116 for further information if needed.

Listening

Part 1

STARTER
Direct students' attention to the photos and the descriptions at the bottom of the page, and ask them to suggest what is happening in each picture and what they think these activities involve. Note any useful vocabulary on the board.

1 Students work in pairs to answer the questions. Encourage them to justify their answers with reasons and examples. Elicit answers from around the class to compare ideas.

2 🔊 06 Go over the instructions with the class before playing the recording. Compare the vocabulary students noted down to help them identify the answer.

> **Answer**
> Roof-top walk
> **Suggested answer**
> words which helped: cool way to see the city's sights, safety, equipment, walking, heights, balance

3 🔊 06 Students try to answer the question on their own from what they remember. Then they listen to the recording again to check their answer.

> **Answer**
> C

4 🔊 06 Students use a copy of the audio script to identify the reasons why each answer is correct or incorrect.

> **Suggested answers**
> 'I personally would have preferred less time standing listening to him, and more time walking.' (C: correct answer)
> 'the guide made sure everyone in our group used the equipment provided properly.' (A: incorrect answer)
> 'thankfully, the guide wasn't taking photos and trying to sell them to you' (B: incorrect answer)

Audio script Track 06
Narrator: You hear a boy talking about going on a tour in a city.
Boy: I did the tour with my older sister, and we both thought it was a really cool way to see the city's sights. It was well organised but in a fairly low-key way – thankfully, the guide wasn't taking photos and trying to sell them to you, for instance. There was nothing low key about the safety, though – the guide made sure everyone in our group used the equipment provided properly. But though he was great, I personally would have preferred less time standing listening to him, and more time walking. The tour's challenging in places, but so long as you have no serious issues with heights or balance, you should be fine.

✓ Exam task

Check whether students are familiar with the format of Listening Part 1. If necessary, ask questions to elicit details. For example, *How many recordings will you hear in the exam?* (eight), *Are the recordings connected to each other?* (no), *How many speakers do you hear in each recording?* (one or two), *How many times do you hear each recording* (twice). You could also take this opportunity to suggest to students that when they read the questions through before listening, they could underline the key words in each question and answer option to help them focus on the main ideas.

Allow students time to read through the questions, and explain any unknown vocabulary. For example, *wild camping* means camping in a remote location rather than on an official campsite with facilities such as water and electricity. In some countries this is illegal. It may also be necessary to explain that *college* is used in the US to refer to a university whereas in the UK it usually refers to an educational institution for students from 16–19 years old.

🔊 07 Play the recording and ask students to complete the task on their own. If possible, they should listen for reasons to exclude the incorrect answer options as well as reasons why they chose the answer they did. Go over the answers with the class, eliciting explanations and justifications for the choices made.

> **Exam task answers**
> 1 C   2 B   3 C   4 C

Audio script Track 07
You will hear people talking in four different situations. For questions 1–4, choose the best answer (A, B or C).
One. You hear a woman on the radio talking about a basketball exhibition centre.
Woman: The College Basketball Experience in Kansas City is a world-class entertainment facility spread over two floors. It contains the National Collegiate Basketball Hall of Fame, where visitors can learn about college basketball legends as well as the history of the game. There are also activity stations, where you can actually practise skills like passing and shooting. For a change of pace, sit and watch the highlights of some top college basketball games. There are also numerous kiosks where you can hear a great range of fascinating information from coaches and players about college basketball.

Two. You hear two friends talking about Disneyland.
Boy: You love Disney films so much! Have you ever been to Disneyland?
Girl: No, it's always been my dream, but I have Disney Days at home.
Boy: What d'you mean?
Girl: Me and my sister spend a day listening to loads of the movie soundtracks and watching our favourite films. Plus, we go online and watch Disneyland parades and go on their rides – virtually, of course. We even sometimes make the snacks you get in Disneyland!
Boy: Wow! So there's no need to go to the actual place, is there?
Girl: Perhaps not!
Boy: But let me know next time you're having a Disney Day, and I'll join you!

Three. You hear two friends talking about wild camping.

Girl:	I went wild camping with my mum last weekend.
Boy:	How's that different from normal camping?
Girl:	It means not on a campsite, in a remote place.
Boy:	You're kidding! With no electricity?
Girl:	Exactly, or water – we had to carry it all with us. But we put our tent up near a lake and had a swim each evening – really refreshing after a day's hiking.
Boy:	Great if you're into that kind of outdoor stuff like you are, but you'll never catch me camping in a tent, miles from civilisation with nowhere to charge my mobile.
Girl:	Mmm, it's pretty hard to imagine you enjoying that!

Four. You hear a boy talking about travelling.

Boy:	I've been brought up to believe that travelling is a good thing, and I've seen that it can teach you a lot about your own life, as well as about the other lives you witness during your visits to other countries. That said, I think our generation has to think again about it because of the damaging effect of international travel on the environment, air travel in particular. I'm not trying to stop us having adventures, though, we just need to find more local ones. Exploring the hidden corners of your own neighbourhood or getting to know other regions of your own country can feel adventurous too.

FURTHER PRACTICE

For further practice put students into groups of three or four and ask them to select one of the topics from the four situations in the recordings to research. Each group then gives a short presentation about their topic to the class. Encourage them to include any personal experience they have and to use dictionaries to look up any useful vocabulary.

Reading and Use of English

Part 2

STARTER

With books closed, write the title *A city boy who lives in a village* on the board and elicit suggestions as to the content of the text. Accept all reasonable answers and note any useful vocabulary on the board.

1 Tell students to open their books, and set a one-minute time limit for them to read the text to check how accurate their suggestions were. Tell students not to worry about the gaps for now. Hold a brief feedback session to compare ideas. Then ask students to reread the text and complete the gaps with the prepositions in the box, explaining that this is the type of language which may be tested in Reading and Use of English Part 2. Students check answers with a partner before class feedback.

Answers
1 up   2 out   3 of   4 up   5 out   6 from   7 on   8 with

2 Students work in pairs to find the phrasal verbs in the text which correspond to the definitions listed. Again, point out that knowledge of phrasal verbs such as these can be helpful in Reading and Use of English Part 2. Check answers as a class.

Answers
1 go out   2 put on   3 end up   4 grow up   5 hang out

☑ Exam task

Before focusing on the exam task, elicit what students know or remember about Reading and Use of English Part 2 and how they might best approach it. Elicit or suggest that it is a good idea to read the title and the text quickly to get a sense of what the main ideas are before thinking about the answers. Go over the exam tip with the class and check understanding. Give students time to complete the task, pointing out that in the exam they should spend around ten minutes on this part. Remind them to read before and after the gap. When everyone has finished, tell them to read the whole text through again to make sure the word they have chosen fits. Check answers as a class and discuss any common mistakes.

Exam task answers
1 where   2 on   3 a   4 many   5 about   6 other   7 not
8 been

FURTHER PRACTICE

If time allows, put students into pairs to make some sentences using the phrasal verbs from Ex 1 and 2.

Part 3

Vocabulary – Word building (1)

3 Focus on the example and elicit sentences from the class using the two adjectives *terrified* and *terrifying* to check understanding. Highlight the spelling differences. Then put students into pairs to continue the exercise. Go through the answers with the whole class, focusing on the differences in pronunciation of the *-ed* ending. If necessary, remind students of the rule that when the word ends *-ted* or *-ded* an extra syllable is added.

Answers

-ed	-ing	-ed or -ing
attached bothered fixed inexperienced	demanding entertaining existing	astonished, astonishing convinced, convincing exhausted, exhausting fascinated, fascinating irritated, irritating terrified, terrifying

4 Give students a few minutes to complete the exercise. Then check answers with the class.

> **Answers**
> 1 exhausting   2 astonished   3 terrified   4 convincing
> 5 irritating

5 If necessary, allow students a minute or two to discuss the question with a partner before checking with the whole class.

> **Answer**
> Adjectives that end in -ed generally describe emotions; they tell us how people feel. Adjectives that end in -ing generally describe the thing that causes the emotion; a boring lesson makes you feel bored.

✓ Exam task

Elicit anything students know or remember about Reading and Use of English Part 3 and read through the exam tips with the class. Draw attention to the photo and the title of the text and ask students what they think the text will be about. Remind them that in the exam the title is there to provide a context and help them predict the content of the text. Give them a minute to skim read the text to check their predictions and get a general idea of the topic before allowing them around ten minutes to complete the task on their own. Remind students to check their answers for spelling before going over them as a whole class, focusing on pronunciation as they answer.

> **Exam task answers**
> 1 childhood   2 scenery   3 fascinating   4 reality
> 5 lifetime   6 unbelievable   7 talented   8 digestion

FURTHER PRACTICE

If time allows, elicit any other words which could be formed from the base words listed in the exam task. For example, childish, childishly, fascinated, realistic. Then ask students to make sentences with some of the words.

Grammar

Adverb formation

1 If necessary, go over the first item with the class checking understanding, and remind students to pay attention to spelling.

> **Answers**
> 1 bitter   2 clumsy   3 happy   4 hopeful   5 miserable
> 6 positive   7 polite   8 rapid   9 rare   10 simple

2 Put students into pairs to complete the exercise before class feedback. Refer students to Grammar reference page 82, as necessary.

> **Answers**
> 1 Adjectives ending in -y change their last letter to -i before adding -ly.
> 2 Adjectives ending in a consonant and -le lose the last letter before adding -y.
> 3 Adjectives ending in -e keep the -e and add -ly.
> 4 Adjectives ending in -l keep the -l and add -ly.

3 This exercise focuses on meaning and collocation. Encourage students to read the whole sentence before choosing the answer, and allow time for them to check their answers with a partner before class feedback. Discuss synonyms of the correct answers to help explain any difficulties.

> **Answers**
> 1 an interesting   2 a courageous   3 a concerning   4 a strong
> 5 a detailed   6 aggressive   7 an excellent   8 a successful

4 Tell students to read the whole sentence before choosing their answers. Ask students to work in pairs to discuss the difference in meaning between the two answer options before choosing the correct one. When going through the answers with the class, elicit example sentences to explain the meaning of the incorrect adverb in each case.

> **Answers**
> 1 calmly   2 positively   3 loudly   4 quickly   5 efficiently
> 6 kindly   7 closely   8 patiently

Past tenses

Before or after the lesson refer students to the QR codes to access Grammar on the Move.

5 Elicit that the past perfect is used to show that an action happened before another action in the past. If necessary, give an example using your own experience, such as Before I got a job in this school, I had worked in two other schools. Refer students to the Grammar reference on page 82, as necessary. Tell them to read the text before putting the verbs into the correct form. Check answers as a class.

> **Answers**
> 1 attempted   2 had reached   3 had travelled   4 went
> 5 had been   6 were   7 hadn't / had not seen   8 flew

6 Tell students to work through this revision task individually before checking their answers with a partner. Encourage them to justify their answers and, if possible, explain why the other option is incorrect. Go over answers with the class.

> **Answers**
> 1 watched   2 got; 'd forgotten   3 finished   4 travelled
> 5 was coming; found   6 was sold
> 7 've been trying; haven't done   8 looked

Writing

Part 2 story

1 Draw attention to the photo and elicit vocabulary from the class to describe what they can see, who they think the person is and where he might be. Then read through the exam task question with the class and explain that the story question always has the same characteristics (the first sentence which must be used is provided along with two content points). Put students into pairs to discuss their predictions about the story using the words and phrases in the box. Elicit suggestions from around the class and then give students a minute or two to read the story in Ex 2 to check their predictions.

2 Ask students to read the story again and choose the correct verb forms. Tell them to discuss their answers with a partner and try to justify their choices, before checking answers as a class.

> **Answers**
> 1 looking (the participle belongs with *I was* and describes a continuous action over a period of time)
> 2 knew (the verb *know* is not used in the continuous form)
> 3 had (past perfect because you are thinking of a period of previous time, before this story starts)
> 4 had built (as 3)
> 5 heard (the verb *hear* is not used in the continuous form)
> 6 realised (the verb *realise* is not used in the continuous form)
> 7 was
> 8 called
> 9 've (present perfect for a very recent action in the past; the plate is probably still in her hand)
> 10 rushed
> 11 was going (continuous action over a period of time)
> 12 disappeared
> 13 didn't
> 14 got out (continuation of story)
> 15 shone (continuation of story)
> 16 'd
> 17 had (past perfect continuous because you are thinking of an action previous to when this story starts)

3 Explain to the class that one aspect of organisation in writing means using paragraphs appropriately. Generally speaking, each new idea or topic should be written in a new paragraph. Tell students to reread the text and to think about what the purpose of each of the three sections is and then to decide where each section starts and ends. Check answers as a class.

> **Answers**
> Paragraph 1 ends after *centuries ago*, and sets the scene for the story.
> Paragraph 2 ends after *disappeared down into a deep hole* and describes the main events of the story.
> Paragraph 3 describes what happened to the writer and what he found.

4 Read through the exam task with the class, eliciting some examples of relatives and buildings to check understanding. Then put students into pairs to brainstorm ideas. Encourage students to note down their ideas and to decide which information they will include in each paragraph at the planning stage. Go through the points on the list with the class, telling them to think about this information as they plan, and to use it as a checklist when they finish writing. Go over the exam tip and elicit some examples of collocations.

☑ Exam task

Allow about 25 minutes for the exam task. If you wish, you could ask students to exchange their story with a partner and give each other some feedback, using the same checklist. Refer students to the Writing bank on page 106 for further information if needed.

> **Model answer**
> When I was walking home from school, I looked up from my phone and realised I didn't recognise the street I was in. So now what? Surprisingly, I didn't feel too worried. The area looked interesting, and I began to walk towards a tall, circular tower at the end of it. As I got nearer, I became more and more convinced I'd seen a picture of it. But where?
> While I was looking up at the tower, an elderly woman suddenly appeared next to me. She was smiling and saying my name. I couldn't believe it! It was Great Aunt Nina! Then I knew where I'd seen the tower before – in a family photo of my grandpa and his sisters.
> 'We lived in this street when we were kids!' Nina said. 'I often come back here. Come on, let's go up the tower!'
> From the top of the tower, I could see my neighbourhood. It wasn't far.
> Nina walked home with me, chatting about her childhood days. Soon we were home, and everyone was delighted to see Aunt Nina, and me of course!

3 Performance

UNIT OBJECTIVES

TOPICS: Music and performing, films and theatre

GRAMMAR: linking words, the passive

VOCABULARY: music, film and cinema

READING AND USE OF ENGLISH PART 7: using context to choose answers

PART 4: understanding the task

WRITING PART 2: a review, organising paragraphs

LISTENING PART 4: listening for details and general understanding, predicting what you might hear

SPEAKING PART 1: giving extended answers

PART 2: avoiding unknown words, expressing preferences

Reading and Use of English

STARTER

Write three headings on the board: *Music genres, Musical instruments* and *People in music*. Ask students to suggest as many words as possible for each category (e.g. *classical, punk, trumpet, singer, violinist, roadie*). Model the pronunciation of any challenging words as necessary.

1 Focus attention on the photos and then allow a few minutes for students to complete the task. Elicit answers from around the class explaining any vocabulary as needed.

> **Answers**
> 1 rap artist, punk rock band   2 drum kit, bass guitar
> 3 guitarist, lead singer   4 microphone, lighting

2 Put students into pairs to discuss their answers to the questions before going over answers with the class. Encourage students to suggest any other words they know which fit in each category and were not already mentioned in the initial brainstorm session.

> **Answers**
> 1 microphone, lighting, cables, speakers   2 drum kit, keyboard, bass guitar, cello   3 orchestra, punk rock band, jazz band, backing group   4 rap artist, conductor, guitarist, lead singer

Part 7

3 Before referring students to the task, elicit or provide some information about Reading and Use of English Part 7.

Ask students what the task looks like and what they have to do. They can look at the exam task on page 23 if they are not sure. Then refer students to the title of the article before allowing them a minute or so to complete the task. Point out that they should just read for gist at this stage and should not worry about the words in bold or the numbers. Check answers as a class.

> **Answers**
> The advantages of being a musician: C
> A summary of what the text is about: A
> The disadvantages of being a musician: B

4 Encourage students to read both before and after the words and phrases in bold to try to understand the meaning from the context before matching them with the definitions. They can discuss their answers with a partner before class feedback.

> **Answers**
> 1 releases a track   2 the beat   3 a passion   4 the lyrics
> 5 the media   6 the critics

5 Read through the phrases in Ex 5 with the class, dealing with any unknown vocabulary and eliciting synonyms or explanations as necessary. Then allow time for students to read the article again to complete the task. Remind students that there may be two answers to a question. Students work individually before comparing their answers in pairs.

> **Answers**
> a 8   b 10   c 1, 2   d 9   e 6, 7   f 3, 4, 5

6 Draw attention to the exam task text and read through the instructions with the class to introduce the topic. Then ask students to scan the text for gist in order to match the sections with the topics. Set a time limit to encourage them to do this fairly quickly.

> **Answers**
> 1 D   2 C   3 E   4 B   5 A

✓ Exam task

Allow students between five and ten minutes to do the exam task under exam conditions, i.e. individually without conferring. Encourage them to underline the sections of the texts which give them the answers, pointing out that this is a good habit to get into so that they can check their answers in the exam more easily. Check answers as a class.

> **Exam task answers**
> 1 C   2 B   3 A   4 B   5 D   6 E   7 C

FURTHER PRACTICE

Put students into small groups to research another job in the arts and find out information about what the job involves, how much the salary usually is, what training or skills are needed, etc. They could then give a short presentation about it to the class.

Listening

STARTER

With books closed, write the heading *Film and theatre* on the board and ask students to name people who work in these sectors and/or their jobs. If they run out of ideas or don't know the vocabulary, encourage them to explain what the person does (e.g. *they write the story for a film*) and check whether anyone else in the class knows the word (*screenwriter*), or to name a person (e.g. *Steven Spielberg*) and elicit their role (*director*).

1 Draw attention to the table and the words in the box, explaining vocabulary as necessary, and then the photos. Put students into pairs to compare and discuss the two situations and make notes in the table, pointing out that some of the words can be used in more than one context. Move around the room and monitor as students work. Elicit feedback from a few different pairs.

> **Answers**
> 1 a play: playwright; a film: screenwriter/scriptwriter
> 2 a play and a film: actors, act scenes, director
> 3 a play and a film: producer
> 4 a play: set designer, scenery painter, costume designer, sound and lighting technicians, stage manager; a film: set designer, costume designer, sound and lighting technicians, camera operator
> 5 a play: in a theatre / on stage, live, by an audience; a film: recorded (on set), in a cinema, by viewers or an audience

2 Students work in pairs to match the words in the box with the nouns in the list. Encourage them to discuss their answers and use dictionaries to check their answers if required. When going over the answers, check pronunciation too.

> **Answers**
> 1 innovation   2 a production   3 a viewer   4 a masterpiece
> 5 a budget   6 an agent   7 a cast   8 an amateur

Part 4

3 Ask the class some questions to find out what they already know about Listening Part 4. For example, *How many recordings do you hear?* (one), *How many times do you hear the recording?* (twice), *How many speakers are there?* (usually two), *How many questions are there?* (seven multiple-choice questions).

Draw attention to the exam task and ask students why they think those words have been underlined (they focus on the most important information). Read the exam tip with the class and point out that in the exam they will have one minute to read through the questions and answer options before they listen to the recording. They should use this time to underline the most important ideas and words and think about what they might hear. Lead a brief class discussion to compare the words which students have underlined and offer guidance as needed on how to identify key ideas.

> **Answers**
> Instructions: interview, a student, how his school helped him get into drama college
> 2 Rowan says that the <u>end-of-year show</u> at the school is <u>intended</u> to
> A <u>appeal equally</u> to <u>professionals</u> and <u>amateurs</u> in the audience.
> B give participants a <u>production experience</u> that is <u>close to professional</u>.
> C achieve a <u>professional standard</u> within a <u>tight budget</u>.
> 3 <u>What view</u> of the <u>technical side</u> of productions was <u>taught</u> at the school?
> A It is a <u>good choice</u> for <u>further education</u>.
> B It is <u>as important</u> as the <u>acting</u>.
> C It is <u>more demanding</u> than it <u>seems</u>.
> 4 <u>What</u> did <u>Rowan appreciate</u> about the school <u>trips</u>?
> A the <u>range of artistic work</u> they exposed him to
> B the <u>focus</u> they had on <u>traditional theatre</u>
> C the <u>opportunity</u> they gave him to <u>see live performances</u>

4 This task encourages students to focus on and predict the content of the recording before they listen, which is a useful skill for the exam. Ask students to reread the instructions and questions, if necessary, in order to choose answers from the list. Students compare answers with a partner before class feedback.

> **Answers**
> Tick: a, c, d, e, f

✅ Exam task

🔊 **08** Play the recording. Students listen to the recording twice and answer the questions on their own, working under exam conditions. When going over the answers with the class try to elicit why the other answer options are wrong in each case.

> **Exam task answers**
> 1 C   2 B   3 B   4 A

FURTHER PRACTICE

Refer students back to the different jobs they discussed in Ex 1 and put them in small groups to talk about why they would or wouldn't like to do those jobs, and what type of course/school they should do / go to to prepare or train for each job. Groups report their ideas to the rest of the class.

Speaking

Part 1

STARTER

Lead a brief class discussion to elicit what students remember about the Speaking test. If necessary, ask them *How many parts are there?* (four), *How long is each part?* (two minutes, four minutes, four minutes, four minutes). Encourage students to say what they have to do in Speaking Part 1 and Part 2.

1 Read the exam tip with the class and then direct attention to question 1 and the example answer. Remind students that they should try to demonstrate how much they know by giving extended answers, if possible. Point out the different parts of the answer indicated by the arrows and then ask two or three students around the class to give their own answers to the question using the same pattern of information. Next, give students time to read and write answers to the rest of the questions, giving extended answers similar to the example. Monitor as students write, offering feedback or support with language as needed.

2 Students work in pairs to ask and answer the questions. More confident students can be asked to give their answers without reading from the page. Finally, ask one or two students to tell the class their answers.

Refer students to the Speaking bank on page 108 for further information if needed.

Part 2

3 Draw attention to the photos and put students into pairs to brainstorm their ideas and make a list using notes.

4 🔊 **09** Play the recording and ask students to tick any ideas on their list that they hear the students mention. Hold a brief feedback session to compare answers.

5 🔊 **09** Give students time to read the phrases before playing the recording again so that they can complete the gaps. Check answers as a class.

Answers
1 devices   2 types   3 black box; name

Examiner:	Pablo, which of these situations would you like to watch a film in?
Pablo:	Er, I'd definitely like to watch a film in both situations. I'd love to go to an outdoor film in a park with my friends; it looks fun – though I wouldn't choose a … well … one of those types of film – and I often watch films or video clips when I'm travelling on a bus or a train.
Examiner:	Thank you. Now, here are your photographs. They show different groups of people playing music. I'd like you to compare the photographs, and say why you think the people in these different groups are playing music.
Pablo:	Well, the first photo shows some teenagers playing guitars in some kind of band. Three of them are playing electric guitars and there's a drum kit with someone playing it. You can't see where they are, but I don't think they're performing at a concert because it's such a small space. It looks to me like they're just playing to have a good time and hang out with their mates. Judging by the expressions on their faces, they don't seem to be taking it too seriously. A lot of people want to play in bands like these because it makes them seem cool – that could be a reason for them playing music like this. The other picture has a very different atmosphere. There are some people playing instruments – guitars. They're connected to a black box for the sound, but I don't know the name of that. The musicians all look very serious. This could be because they're playing to earn a living, so it's important to them. Or they could be students who need some extra money. Alternatively, perhaps they're raising money for a charity. It's certainly not just about having fun.
Examiner:	Thank you. Anna, which of the activities would you prefer to do?
Anna:	Mmm … that's a difficult choice because I'd sooner not do either of them. I'm just not musical! But I guess if I had to do one of them, I'd rather play in the band because I'm really into rock music.
Examiner:	Thank you.

6 Read the instructions with the class. Explain that students should use one of the phrases in Ex 5, or a suitable alternative, to explain the meaning of the words in the box. Students work in pairs.

7 🔊 **10** Remind students that when the one minute is up they will have up to 30 seconds to answer a question about their partner's photos. Play the recording and ask students to tick the phrases they hear.

> **Answers**
> Tick: I'd rather; I'd sooner

Audio script Track 10

Examiner:	Pablo which of these situations would you like to watch a film in?
Pablo:	Er, I'd definitely like to watch a film in both situations. I'd love to go to an outdoor film in a park with my friends; it looks fun – though I wouldn't choose a … well … one of those types of film – and I often watch films or video clips when I'm travelling on a bus or a train.
Examiner:	Anna, which of the activities would you prefer to do?
Anna:	Mmm … that's a difficult choice because I'd sooner not do either of them. I'm just not musical! But I guess if I had to do one of them, I'd rather play in the band because I'm really into rock music.

✅ Exam task

Ask students to work with a different partner to practise the exam task. Remind them of the information in the exam tip, and to use some of the phrases in Ex 5 and Ex 7. Tell the listening partner to check the timing but point out that in the exam students will not be able to look at the clock so they should use this opportunity to get used to what it feels like to speak for around one minute. Tell the listening partner not to speak until the one minute is up so that the speaking partner knows they have more time and should continue speaking, as would happen in the exam. Ask some students around the class for feedback to discuss what they found most challenging. For example, were they able to speak for one minute or did they run out of ideas? Did they use some of the phrases suggested? Did they have difficulty finding words or were they able to paraphrase? For extra practice students can repeat the task, and speak about the other photo.

Refer students to the Speaking bank on page 110 for further information if needed.

Writing

Part 2 review

> **STARTER**
> With books closed, lead a brief brainstorm session to elicit as many different types of film as possible. Note any new vocabulary on the board. Then put students into small groups to discuss what their favourite genres are and to give some examples of the films they have enjoyed recently.

1 Ask students to open their books and check the list to see if there are any they didn't mention. Students do the exercise on their own and compare their answers with a partner. Conduct a quick survey by asking students to raise their hands to see which are the most popular types of film across the class.

Then read question 2 and the answer options in the box with the class, checking understanding, and then put students into pairs to discuss their answers. Elicit feedback from one or two pairs and ask other students whether they agree or disagree and why.

2 Remind the class that in Writing Part 2 they have a choice of questions. Elicit which type of text they may be asked to write (story, review, article or informal letter/email). Tell them that they are going to read a model answer for a review today. Ask students to read the exam task, without worrying about the gaps for now, and go over the answers to the questions together.

> **Answers**
> 1 Yes – genre not specified
> 2 Yes – 'whether you would recommend it' allows for not recommending

3 Read through the questions with the class and then ask them to read the review. Ask them to underline the parts of the text which give the answers. Students discuss their answers with a partner before class feedback.

> **Answers**
> 1 Yes (coming-of-age, fantasy element, clever twists and turns, struggling to make decisions, etc.)
> 2 Students' own answers
> 3 Present tense. Past tense could be used, but present tense is usually used in reviews to make the story more engaging.

4 Go through the information in the table and give students a few minutes to reread the text to complete the task.

> **Answers**
> a description of what happens in the film: Paragraph 2
> the reviewer's recommendation: Paragraph 3
> a summary of the effect of the film: Paragraph 3
> what kind of film it is: Paragraph 1

5 Students work in pairs to answer the question. Encourage them to find the phrases used in the text for each of the aspects mentioned and then to talk about the meaning.

> **Answers**
> the plot, the main character, the overall effect of the film, the animations, the type of film

6 Finally, students complete the gaps with the appropriate words. If necessary, ask them to say which words are used to introduce a contrasting idea, which are used to give an example, and which to add extra information, before rereading the words around each gap to make their choice.

> **Answers**
> 1 Although   2 such as   3 However   4 also

✓ Exam task

Read the instructions with the class, reminding them that in the exam they have a choice of questions to answer in Writing Part 2 but there will not be more than one question for each type of text as there is here. Give students time to read the two questions and deal with any queries. Point out that the only difference between the two questions is the genre of film which has to be described. Go over the checklist and tell students to use this when planning but also when checking their writing after they finish. Regarding the word count, tell students that they should try to write at least 170 words in order to demonstrate a range and variety of language and to fully answer each part of the question. Allow around 35 minutes for students to write their reviews on their own and then another five minutes for checking. Students could exchange their writing with a partner for peer feedback or hand it in for correction. Refer students to the Writing bank on page 100 for further information if needed.

> **Model answers**
> **The best thriller ever: Bullitt**
> I saw this old film again recently on DVD and it's still fantastic. It stars Robert Vaughan as an ambitious politician who wants to fight organised crime, and Steve McQueen as Bullitt, one of the detectives whose job is to protect him. The film has a very complicated plot. Bullitt has to be very clever to catch the criminals and stop the politician from being murdered.
> The film is still famous after many years because it has some amazing action scenes, with Bullitt driving a green Ford Mustang car. The most famous scene is a car chase, with two bad guys chasing Bullitt up the hills in San Francisco. They go everywhere, including up and down the steps that San Francisco is famous for. It's so exciting it takes your breath away! The other great chase is at the airport, on the runways. It's amazing.
> I would definitely recommend this film. In my opinion, it is outstanding. It makes you feel as if you are experiencing what is going on. You will enjoy it because the action scenes keep you on the edge of your seat.
>
> **Romantic comedy: One Day**
> This is a very interesting story because of the way it is told. The two main characters, Dexter and Emma, meet at university and become best friends. They both get romantically involved with other people, and there are lots of amusing moments. The film explains how their lives turn out by showing you what happens over the years on just one day each year.
> There are big highs and lows in this film. At first you think Dexter and Emma will never get together, but in the end they do, and for a while they are incredibly happy. But then the film changes; it all ends in tragedy, and Dexter is nearly destroyed as a person, until his father is able to rescue him and show him how to get on with his life and make a new start.
> I really like it; the ending is very unusual for a romantic comedy. It's not what you expect at all, which I think is one of the best things about the film. I'd recommend anyone who enjoys romantic comedies to see this film.

Grammar

Linking words

Before or after the lesson refer students to the QR code to access *Grammar on the Move*.

1 Give students plenty of time to find the linking words in the text on page 22. Put them into pairs to discuss how each word is used, highlighting what type of words follow it, for example, and what the meaning is. Deal with any queries they have before asking them to complete the task. Point out that in some sentences there is more than one correct answer. Go over the answers with the class, highlighting the grammar and meaning of each word as needed. Refer students to the Grammar reference on page 84 as necessary.

> **Answers**
> 1 In spite of   2 However,   3 However,   4 Even though /
> Although   5 even though / although   6 In spite of

The passive

Before or after the lesson refer students to the QR code to access *Grammar on the Move*.

2 Refer students to page 84 in the Grammar reference as needed. Go over the first sentence with the class, checking understanding and eliciting or explaining, if necessary, that the passive is often used when we want to show that the event or action is more important than the person or thing which caused it. Students can work individually or in pairs before class feedback.

> **Answers**
> 1 My bedroom was cleaned while I was asleep!   2 Lots of bargains can be found on this app.   3 My date of birth had been given to the school secretary. / The school secretary had been given my date of birth.   4 It is thought that protesters are to blame for the graffiti.   5 My wallet has been stolen!
> 6 The colour of all the classroom walls is being changed.
> 7 You will be given a camera to use on the film course.

3 Refer back to the sentences in Ex 2 and point out that each sentence uses a different verb form or tense. Elicit that sentence 6 uses the present continuous and go over the example answers in the table before giving students a few minutes to complete the table with a partner. Check answers as a class.

> **Answers**
> present simple: is thought
> present continuous: is being changed
> future simple: will be given
> past simple: was cleaned
> present perfect: has been stolen
> past perfect: had been given
> with modals: can be found

4 Explain that exam candidates often make mistakes when using passive forms, and that it is good practice for students to learn to spot this type of mistake when checking their own work, if possible. Allow time for students to work through the task before checking their answers with a partner. Go through the answers when everyone has finished.

> **Answers**
> 1 These days everything ~~has been running~~ **is run** by computers.   2 I was show**n** a brochure which contained some exciting holiday destinations.   3 The club **was** first founded in 1886.   4 Will food **be** provide**d** / **Is** food provide**d** in the price of the school trip?   5 My mother **is** called Naomi.   6 The show **was** supposed to start at 6.00, but the actor was ill.   7 The park **is** located in a beautiful part of London.   8 The museum tour **was** arranged a month ago.   9 This cathedral ~~has been builded~~ **was built** in the early 14th century.   10 My parents have a holiday home that **is** situated just one mile from the beach.

Reading and Use of English

Part 4

STARTER
Initiate a brief class discussion by asking students to say what they remember about Reading and Use of English Part 4 and elicit any strategies they can think of which can be helpful in this part.

1 Point out that changing a sentence from active to passive or vice versa is an example of what may be tested in Reading and Use of English Part 4.

Focus attention on the information given and ask one or two questions to check understanding, for example, *How many words do you have to write in your answer?* (between two and five words), *What must you include?* (the word given). Go over the example with the class and ask them to work in pairs to match the comments with the answer options. When checking answers explain that these are typical mistakes that exam candidates make.

> **Answers**
> A 4   B 1   C 2   D 3

2 Tell students that there are two possible marks for each answer, which means that there are usually two changes that have to be made from the original sentence. This also means that in the exam, if they are unsure of the answer, they should always make an attempt as they could potentially get one mark if at least one part of their answer is correct. Ask students to discuss the answers with a partner before class feedback.

> **Answers**
> 1 Because it follows 'To everyone's', a noun is required.
> 2 It has changed from an active form (*the head teacher cancelled*) to a passive form (*the trip was cancelled by*).

3 Draw attention to the example sentences and put students into pairs to discuss their answers to the questions. Explain that these are the types of questions they should ask themselves to help complete the answers in the exam. Elicit answers from around the class.

> **Answers**
> 1 supposed   2 Passive – the school concert is not an active subject; people supposed this.   3 infinitive   4 be – over is an adverb meaning finish

✓ Exam task

Read through the exam tip with the class before allowing students 15 minutes to complete the exam task. Advise students to look back at the original sentence when checking their answers to make sure they have included all the ideas and that the second sentence has the same meaning. They should also check they haven't written more than five words in their answers. When checking answers encourage students to explain the steps they took to get to the answers and ask them to try to identify the part of each answer which is worth each mark.

> **Exam task answers**
> 1 in spite of (his) | feeling/being
> 2 will be built/constructed/erected | next/adjacent
> 3 is (being) / has been criticised/criticized | by
> 4 as soon as | it
> 5 be released | in
> 6 come up with | a

4 Fit and healthy

Reading and Use of English

STARTER

Introduce the topic by eliciting from the class the names of sports they enjoy playing and those they prefer watching, asking them to justify their answers with reasons.

1 Draw attention to the photo and give students a few minutes to answer the questions in pairs. Then go over the answers with the class.

> **Answers**
> 1 a football, b soccer
> 2 The man in a light-blue shirt. The ref.
> 3 The ref is talking to one of the players, possibly because he gave a bad tackle to one of his opponents.
> 4 Students' own answers

2 Give students a few minutes to do the task with a partner. When going over answers elicit or provide any other vocabulary to describe the photo. For example, *goal, net, goalposts, the crowd/fans/supporters*. It may be necessary to explain that *goalie* is a more informal word than *goalkeeper*. Ask students if they know the names of other positions in football apart from *defender* and *goalkeeper* (e.g. *striker, winger*, etc).

> **Answers**
> Circle: defender, spectator, goalkeeper, pitch, goal scorer, goalie, shin guards
> Goalkeeper and goalie mean the same thing.

3 Elicit answers from the class and elicit or explain any unknown words.

> **Answers**
> Court, umpire and fault are all from tennis.

Part 5

4 Tell students to read the introduction, the title and the text to answer the question. Set a time limit of one or two minutes to encourage them to read quickly for gist without worrying about understanding details at this stage. Check answers with the class, eliciting the justifications for their choice.

> **Answers**
> A a novel
> It tells a story, is written in the first person, and is very descriptive.

5 Read through the exam tip with the class explaining that they often have to infer meaning to identify the correct answers to the questions in the exam. Give students time to read the questions and find the answers in the text. Ask them to discuss their ideas with a partner before class feedback.

> **Answers**
> 1 *my watch pointed at three fifteen. I was late. I ran the rest of the way to Parque Yrigoyen field.*
> 2 B by describing what she did

6 Read through the question and answer options with the class and then allow students a few minutes to identify the part of the text which gives the answer. Encourage students to use the information to eliminate any incorrect answers and to use the words they understand in the text to select the answer. Note that students may not know the expression *killer glare* but should be able to use the context to infer that her best friend was annoyed with her as she *took the last place in line* and then the *rest of the girls dispersed*. Point out that this type of deduction is a useful and important skill to develop.

> **Answer**
> B – *Roxana, our goalie and my best friend, sent me a killer glare*

7 Read questions 2 and 5 with the class, checking understanding, and then allow time for students to underline the information in the text. Check answers as a class.

> **Answers**
> 2: *Every time Coach talked about some of us girls going pro, I wanted to believe her. But to hide my ridiculous dreams I laughed dismissively.*
> 5: *She walked away before I could explain that she was asking too much, that I was just a girl with strong legs and a stubborn streak. There is no time for drama, though. I wrapped the band around my arm and did a quick warm up on my own.*

☑ Exam task

Students should be encouraged to read the rest of the questions, underlining any key ideas, before rereading the text to find the answers. Tell them to underline the parts of the text that give the answers, so that they can easily explain their answers and, when in the exam, check them more quickly.

Set a time limit of around ten minutes for students to complete the task before checking answers together.

> **Exam task answers**
> 1 B   2 A   3 A   4 D   5 B

FURTHER PRACTICE

Put students into pairs or small groups to discuss what they think might happen next in the story. They could write a paragraph in their groups and then read it out to the rest of the class.

Listening

Part 2

STARTER

Elicit anything students know or remember about Listening Part 2. If necessary, ask them some questions to elicit details. For example, *How many people do you hear on the recording?* (one), *How many gaps are there to complete in the exam?* (ten), *How many words can you write in each gap?* (one to three), etc.

1 Explain that in the exam students have 45 seconds to read through the task before they listen, and they should use this time to think about the type of word which is missing from each gap. They should use clues and information before and after the gap to help them decide whether they are listening for a singular or plural noun, an adjective, a number, a date, etc. In the exam it is important that they then listen carefully to make sure they choose the correct number, for example, as there may be more than one mentioned.

Put students into pairs to work through the exercise before checking answers as a class.

> **Answers**
> 1   a singular noun: 2, 4
> 2   a plural noun: 3
> 3   a number: 1

2 Give students a few minutes to choose the words which could fit in each gap. Point out that there is more than one answer for each gap and they will be able to choose the correct word only after listening to the recording. Go through answers with the class.

> **Answers**
> 1   12, 15
> 2   diving, table tennis
> 3   responsibilities, injuries
> 4   memory, recovery

3 🔊 **11** Go over the instructions with the class before playing the recording. Compare the vocabulary students noted down to help them identify the answers.

> **Answers**
> 1   12
> 2   table tennis
> 3   injuries
> 4   recovery

> **Audio script Track 11**
> In many sports, the top achievers seem to get younger and younger. But this seems to be particularly true in skateboarding. At the 2020 Olympics in Tokyo, the winning female skateboarders ranged from 12 to 16 years old. So they'd only been alive to see two or three Olympics and then they were in them!
>
> The youngest athlete at the Tokyo Olympics was not in skateboarding, though, or even gymnastics, a sport young teenagers often do extremely well in. It was in fact a young woman called Hend Zaza, a table-tennis player from Syria.
>
> So why do these young people do so well compared to older competitors? Well, one important reason is the fact that they haven't had as many injuries so they don't worry so much about taking risks.
>
> Another advantage that young teenagers have relates to speed of learning new tricks – but not the speed at which a young person's memory can store new information, but how they learn physically. Nobody can learn new skateboarding tricks without pain, and the younger you are, the less time your recovery takes. So kids can carry on skateboarding with little or no pause, and therefore learn more quickly.

☑ Exam task

Go over the instructions and the exam tip, pointing out that the recording here is shorter than in the exam and there are fewer questions. Regarding the exam tip, students need to understand that they will not have to change the form of the words they hear to fit the text. Allow about 30 or 40 seconds for students to read the sentences and try to identify the type of information which fits each gap, and then play the recording. Repeat the recording before checking answers as a class.

Audio script Track 12

You will hear part of a presentation about a young skateboarder called Sky Brown. For questions 1–6, complete the sentences with a word or short phrase.

Sky Brown's a world-famous skateboarder who competed in her first Olympics when she was just 13. Although she's now based in the USA, she also spends a good amount of time in Japan, where she was born and lived for the first few years of her life. That's because she has a mum who's Japanese. Despite all that, she competed in the 2020 Tokyo Olympics for the British team as her dad's originally from England.

Sky says she has no memory of the first time she went on a skateboard because she was so young. However, she does admit she was greatly inspired by her dad, a very keen, very skilled skateboarder. She'd watch him and his friends riding their boards in the backyard whenever she could. But Sky tells reporters that for many years now, she's been picking up all her latest tricks from online videos. The idea of having a coach doesn't seem to have crossed her mind.

Sky's rise to fame began in 2012, at just four years old. Her dad posted some images of her skateboarding on his social media page, and they got millions of views overnight. A few years later, in 2016, she competed in her first event and did so well that she's been competing professionally ever since. Possibly the peak of her fame came in 2018, when she entered a dancing competition on TV and won!

Although still so young, it seems Sky's done it all. On top of her skateboarding achievements, she has over 800,000 followers on social media, and a sponsorship deal with a sportswear brand, which means she appears in their ads. She's also been a recording artist, releasing the pop single 'Girl' in 2020 while she was recovering from a serious fall. And she's even published a book called *Sky's the limit*.

As well as all that, Sky has a full daily routine. She normally gets up at 5 a.m. and, when at home in California, goes surfing nearby. As the skills required are similar to skateboarding, she thinks it helps her sport. After breakfast she does schoolwork online most days, but twice a week in school, and then heads to the skatepark for three to four hours. Her hobbies also include playing the guitar and computer games.

When asked by reporters what dreams she still has, Sky says she wants to keep on travelling around the world, skating and doing her other hobbies with help and guidance from her parents. But she's also motivated by the idea she could be an inspiration for other girls and boys. She says she wants them to see her and think, 'If that small girl of 13 can do it, so can I!'

Speaking

Part 3

1 Hold a brief brainstorming session to elicit what students remember about Speaking Part 3 before focusing attention on the photos and the questions. Allow two or three minutes for pairs to discuss their ideas, encouraging them to justify their answers with reasons and explanations. Ask some pairs to report their opinions to the class.

☑ Exam task

2 Go over the useful expressions and point out that students should try to use a range of expressions rather than repeating one or two. Focus attention on the exam task and elicit or remind the class that in the exam they will be asked to discuss their answers to the first question for two minutes and then they will have one minute to discuss the second question. For this task you could, if you wish, ask students to speak for a little longer than two minutes to give them the opportunity to practise using the useful expressions and discussing as many of the ideas as possible. For the second phase it is probably more useful for them to stick to the one minute they will have in the exam as it requires some skill to be able to complete the task effectively in the time provided. Students need to ensure they express their own opinion and allow enough time for their partner to agree or disagree with them. They need to learn to be aware of timing and try to speak for approximately the same amount of time as their partner. Students should be encouraged to ask questions and use the language provided to react to their partner's ideas rather than just taking turns to speak.

Monitor the pairs as they do the task. Before giving the class your feedback, it might be helpful to ask students to reflect on how well they think they did by asking some questions, for example, *Did you use a variety of expressions from the lists? Did you speak for a similar amount of time to your partner? Did you ask each other questions? Did you give reasons for your opinions?* etc.

Refer students to the Speaking bank on page 114 for further information if needed.

Part 4

3 Go over the question and opinions with the class, checking understanding. Put students into pairs or elicit answers from around the class to discuss whether they agree or disagree with the opinions given. Point out that in Part 4 there is no correct answer. Students will be assessed on their use and range of language, organisation and pronunciation and not on their opinions.

Elicit any other answers to the question from the class, encouraging students to justify their answers with reasons.

☑ Exam task

Read the exam tip with the class, pointing out that students do not need to worry about the timing in Part 4. They should try to give extended answers with reasons but should stop speaking when they have finished their thought. Encourage students to take turns to be the first one to answer each question and then to say whether they agree or disagree with what their partner said and why. To conclude, ask one or two pairs to tell the class their answers.

Refer students to the Speaking bank on page 116 for further information if needed.

Reading and Use of English

Part 2

1 If students are not familiar with this part of the exam, focus attention on the exam task and point out the instructions, which say how many words to write in each gap (one), the title, which provides a context, and the topic (healthy food, takeaways), as well as the number of gaps (eight).

Then read through the instructions to Ex 1 with the class. Put students into pairs to do the task, reminding them to say why the answer given is wrong before they write the correct answers.

Go through answers with the class.

> **Answers**
> 1 Meaning is wrong. It doesn't make sense with 'eat regularly', plus it's not a grammar word (lexis). Correct answer: not
> 2 Wrong spelling. Correct answer: rather
> 3 Wrong type of word. An auxiliary is needed to form the imperative. Correct answer: Do
> 4 Wrong kind of comparative. It needs to go with 'harder'. Correct answer: than
> 5 It should not be the passive. It should be the present perfect. Correct answer: have/'ve
> 6 Two words. The answers have to be one word only. Correct answer: and

2 Students work individually before checking answers with a partner. When checking answers point out that students should look for clues that the word missing is part of a phrase, such as prepositions or other words before and/or after the gap.

> **Answers**
> 1 instead
> 2 addition
> 3 long
> 4 account
> 5 order
> 6 well

✓ Exam task

Go over the exam tip explaining that reading the whole text before they think about the missing words will give them a better idea of the context and the topic, so can help when they are thinking about the answers. Allow students ten minutes to complete the task on their own before class feedback.

> **Exam task answers**
> 1 are   2 as   3 there   4 instead   5 If   6 such   7 rather   8 that/which

> **FURTHER PRACTICE**
> Students talk to a partner about whether they enjoy eating healthy food. They should try to use some of the fixed phrases from Ex 2 and the exam task.

Part 3

Vocabulary – Word building (2)

> **STARTER**
> With books closed write the word *happy* on the board and ask students how many other words they can make by adding prefixes and suffixes. You should be able to elicit *happily, happiness, unhappy, unhappily, happier, happiest* by asking them for the noun, adverb, comparative adjective, etc.

3 Go over the example with the class and ask students to complete the task individually before checking their answers with a partner. Check answers, pointing out that the spelling changes shown are common, but there are also other patterns. If time allows you could ask students if they can think of any. For example, *compete/competitor/competition, concentrate/concentration, argue/argument*, etc.

> **Answers**
> unhappiness   y + iness
> completion   e + ion
> consumer   + r

4 Read through the exam tip with the class reminding them to think about spelling when they do the task. They can work on their own before checking answers with a partner. Go through the answers with the class, checking both spelling and pronunciation of the words.

> **Answers**
> craziness, confidence, laziness, convenience, friendliness lecturer, calculation, manufacturer, association, user, creation

✓ Exam task

Remind students to read the title and the whole text quickly before thinking about the answers. You may need to point out that not all the answers are nouns and students should think about what type of word fits in each gap before transforming the word at the end of the line. Give students around ten minutes to complete the task individually. Check answers as a class, focusing on spelling and pronunciation.

Vocabulary – Health care

5 Put students into pairs to make nouns from the words in the box. With a less confident group you may want to check these as a class before students choose which sentence each word fits into. Encourage students to use dictionaries for this task to check meaning as well as changes in pronunciation in words such as *breathe/breath*. Go over the answers with the class.

Answers
1 breaths
2 infection
3 addiction
4 treatment
5 consciousness
6 disabilities
7 injuries
8 sicknesses

Grammar

Modal verbs

Before or after the lesson refer students to the QR codes to access *Grammar on the Move*.

1 You may want to elicit the functions of the different modal verbs in the box (obligation, permission, advice, etc.) or refer students to the Grammar reference notes on page 85 before putting them into pairs to do the exercise. Check answers as a class.

Answers
1 should
2 can't
3 can
4 have to
5 should have been
6 must have been rehearsing
7 could have lost

2 Give students a few minutes to refer back to the sentences in Ex 1 to match the expressions. Students discuss their answers with a partner before class feedback.

Answers
a 3 (can)
b 6 (must have)
c 1 (should)
d 2 (can't)
e 7 (could have)
f 4 (have to)
g 5 (should have)

3 Students do the task on their own before referring to the Grammar reference on page 85 to check their answers. Elicit answers from around the class and if possible, explanations for the answers.

Answers
1 don't have to
2 had to
3 must
4 must
5 should
6 mustn't

Prepositions: *at, in, on*

4 **5** Give students a few minutes to do the exercises individually before checking answers as a class. Make sure students make a note of any mistakes they make so that they can learn from them. Refer students to the Grammar reference on page 87 as necessary.

Answers
4
1 They waited patiently ~~on~~ **at** the back door for him to come back.
2 They had to wait all afternoon ~~at~~ **in** the queue for the opera tickets.
3 That snake is reputed to be the most poisonous ~~on~~ **in** the world.
4 Correct
5 Correct
6 The facilities ~~in~~ **on** that cruise ship are incredible.
5
1 at   2 at   3 in   4 in   5 in   6 on

Writing

Part 2 email / letter

1 Remind students that in Writing Part 2 they may have to write an email or letter. It could be formal or informal in style, but in this unit they will practise language for an informal piece of writing to a friend.

Give students a few minutes to read the exam question and then elicit one or two example pieces of advice using the different phrases suggested to check students understand how to use them. Then put students into pairs to brainstorm some more advice. Encourage them to use the range of expressions for giving their advice and point out that if they run out of ideas, they could say which sport they do not recommend and why. Elicit some more suggestions from around the class to compare ideas.

2 Explain that this is an example answer to Alex's email from Alex's friend, Pete. Encourage students to read the whole text quickly for general understanding before they complete the gaps with the phrases given. Check answers as a class.

> **Answers**
> 1 don't worry too much about
> 2 remember that
> 3 it should
> 4 it'd be better to
> 5 I suggest you
> 6 Why not
> 7 recommend doing
> 8 you can

3 Put students into pairs to look for the answers in Pete's email. Encourage them to underline the examples in the email where appropriate. Go over the answers with the class, eliciting and highlighting examples in the text.

> **Answers**
> 1 T
> 2 F (He talks about all three.)
> 3 F
> 4 T
> 5 F (He wishes him luck.)
> 6 T (The style is fairly informal, i.e. it's direct, and Pete uses short forms, but the email doesn't contain lots of slang or idioms; it's grammatically correct.)

☑ Exam task

4 If necessary, refer students to the Writing bank on page 98 before giving them a few minutes to read the exam task. Point out that the checklist states they should make sure they understand the whole situation. This means reading the email and identifying who they need to write to and the question(s) they need to answer. The second point on the checklist tells students to plan. In this case that means thinking about ideas for the advice they can give Sam. Refer students to the exam tip and then put students into pairs to make suggestions, remembering to use the phrases from Ex 1 and any other relevant functional language they know. Monitor and offer support with vocabulary as needed. Elicit some suggestions from around the class and note any useful language on the board.

5 Students should refer to the other points on the checklist before they start writing their email. If the class needs extra support, you could briefly brainstorm useful expressions for starting and ending their writing, or ask students to refer back to the emails in Ex 1 and 2 for examples.

Allow around 35 minutes for students to write their email and make sure they check it carefully before handing it in for correction or to a partner for peer feedback.

> **Model answer**
> Hello Sam
> It sounds as though you are in a difficult situation. I know you've always loved football, but I know you are also a good drum player, so it's a tough choice. But actually, I wonder if you have to choose?
> There will probably be football matches every week, but I'm sure you will only have concerts once or twice a term and you'll know in advance when they are going to be. If that's right, why don't you explain the situation to your football coach, and ask if it's OK if you miss a match occasionally? There are always other players who can take your place, aren't there, so perhaps he will be OK with the idea? If that's no good, then you'll have to make a choice. You know I'd always choose sport; it keeps you fit, and you make lots of friends in the team. And as you know, I'm not at all musical. But for you, I don't know – maybe just do whichever will make you happier. And if everything else fails, toss a coin!
> Good luck with it.
> All the best,
> Pieter

Lessons learnt

UNIT OBJECTIVES

TOPICS: achievements, education

GRAMMAR: conditionals

VOCABULARY: phrasal verbs, careers, education

READING AND USE OF ENGLISH PART 1: multiple-choice cloze

PART 4: key-word transformations

PART 7: multiple matching

WRITING PART 2: article, keeping the reader's attention, describing and linking

LISTENING PART 2: sentence completion

SPEAKING PART 1: discussing ambitions, achievements and education

PART 2: comparing photos

Reading and Use of English

STARTER

Ask the class if they have any hobbies or interests outside school which involve particular personal qualities or skills. Hold a brief discussion to generate some vocabulary and interest in the different skills students have. If necessary, you could initiate the discussion by talking about something you do.

1 Focus attention on the photos and elicit answers to the question from around the class. Try to elicit some vocabulary to describe what can be seen in the photos by asking: *What are the people doing/holding? Where are they?* etc.

> **Answers**
> A gardener
> B construction worker
> C code writer
> D sports coach

2 Ask students what personal qualities a gardener needs. Try to elicit one or two before pointing out the table and the information provided. Put students into pairs to briefly discuss how much they agree with it. Elicit feedback from around the class.

3 Allow time for students to discuss and, if you wish, complete the table either by copying it into their exercise books or by using different colours for the other three jobs. When they have finished, lead a brief class discussion to compare ideas, encouraging students to justify their opinions with reasons and explanations.

4 Give students time to complete the sentences using the qualities from the table. Students compare their answers with a partner before class feedback.

> **Answers**
> 1 courage
> 2 honesty
> 3 physical strength
> 4 the capacity to inspire others
> 5 wisdom
> 6 politeness
> 7 willingness to learn
> 8 understanding of others
> 9 creativity
> 10 enthusiasm

Part 7

✓ Exam task

Draw attention to the exam task and elicit anything students remember about Reading and Use of English Part 7. Encourage students to say why it is important to read the instructions, the title and the sub heading before reading the texts (so that they have an idea of the topic and what they are going to read). Read through the exam tip with the class and point out that it can be helpful to underline the key words in the questions as well as the sections of text which give the answers so that they can quickly check their work. Point out that in the exam, students should spend around ten minutes on this part, so they need to learn to read quickly, using skimming and scanning techniques (to get a general idea of the message of the text and then to read the sentences which give the answers more carefully) as they won't have time to read every part of each text in detail.

Set a time limit of around ten minutes and then ask students to discuss their answers with a partner, explaining exactly where they found each answer. Go over the answers with the class, asking them to read out the part of the text which gives the answer.

> **Exam task answers**
> 1 C   2 B   3 D   4 A   5 C   6 D   7 A   8 C   9 A   10 B

FURTHER PRACTICE

Put students into pairs to discuss which of the projects described in the text they would prefer to take part in and why. Follow up with a brief class discussion about any volunteering experiences the students or any of their friends or family have had.

Listening

STARTER

With books closed ask students to imagine they are describing their school to a student from another school. What can they say about the outdoor space and facilities? What other outdoor facilities would they like to have? Elicit or provide vocabulary to describe the outdoor areas (e.g. playground, garden, running track, basketball court, etc.).

1 Draw attention to the photos and elicit or provide some useful vocabulary to describe what can be seen. For example, *amphitheatre*, *sports pitch*. Then put students into pairs to discuss their answers to the questions. Elicit feedback from around the class to compare opinions.

> **Answers**
> 1 They are: painting the chicken house, playing football, listening to a teacher/lecture in an amphitheatre / a theatre
> 2 For example: learning about animals, keeping fit, learning team skills, learning about theatres
> 3 Student's own answers.

Part 2

2 Elicit anything students remember about Listening Part 2. Remind or inform them, if necessary, that students should try to predict the answers (or at least the type of word that would fit in each gap) as they read through the text before listening. Explain that this task helps students practise the predicting part, but obviously in the exam they are not given answer options as here.

Ask students to complete the task and then explain their answers to a partner. Elicit answers from around the class.

> **Answers**
> 1 prawns (You can't grow prawns, and wouldn't breed them in a greenhouse.)
> 2 beef (Beef is a kind of meat, not an animal.)
> 3 musical (A farm wouldn't teach musical skills.)

3 🔊 **13** Read the instructions with the class, checking understanding before playing the recording. Repeat the recording for students to check their answers before going over them as a class.

> **Answers**
> 1 aubergines
> 2 chickens
> 3 practical

> **Audio script Track 13**
> Here at Castle School where I'm a teacher, we've created a tiny farm for the benefit of our students and the local community. Inside our greenhouse, we're able to grow crops like aubergines, and outside we grow various fruit crops, such as cherries. Students involved in running the farm are also keen to get some animals. At the moment, we only have a few chickens, but soon we'll be ready to get some goats too. The purpose of the farm was originally to provide training in practical skills for students who want to work on farms or in the field of science. But students are also learning a wide range of social skills on the school farm as they work with each other, the teachers and parents who are involved.

✓ Exam task

🔊 **14** Read through the exam tips with the class. Remind students that they will hear the exact word or words they need to write although the sentence will not be exactly the same. Refer students to the task they just listened to for some examples of each tip.

Allow time for students to read through the instructions and the text. Remind students that they have 45 seconds to read the task before the recording plays in the exam. Encourage them to try to predict the type of word or words that fit each gap and to read carefully before and after the gaps to make sure that their answers fit grammatically.

Play the recording. Then check answers with the class.

> **Exam task answers**
> 1 football
> 2 competitions
> 3 insects
> 4 pond
> 5 sculpture
> 6 exercise
> 7 ship
> 8 designed
> 9 (nearby) hills
> 10 concerts

> **Audio script Track 14**
> *You will hear a student called Katya giving a presentation at a school council meeting about improving their school's outdoor area. For questions 1–10, complete the sentences with a word or short phrase.*
>
> Katya: Hello, Student Councillors. So, I've done some research and now I'm going to tell you about what four other schools across the country have done in their outdoor areas, and then afterwards, we can discuss which ones we think might work best for our school.
>
> I'll start with the skatepark at Prince's School. They built this a couple of years ago, on a piece of land that used to be a football pitch. This was often out of use because of wet weather, so children ended up just playing basketball in their school hall. Now they have the skatepark for exercise in most weathers. One of the other great benefits of the skatepark, the school says, is that it's created stronger links with the community, as skateboarders of all ages and from all over the local area come to competitions held at the school. They're also planning to invite top skaters to come and give demonstrations – which, as well as being great for learning, might also be a good way to raise money.

Next, I'll tell you about the new wildlife garden at The Kite School. There, students have planted a wide selection of wild flowers to attract as many insects as possible – some student photographers have posted pictures of it and it looks lovely. They've also planted vegetables in large wooden containers, and in one corner they've put a pond which is now home to lots of wild creatures like frogs and flies. The birds also drink from it, and one early morning a teacher even spotted a fox having a drink there. The students of The Kite School have got all kinds of plans for the future of the wildlife garden, too. For example, there's a group of trees in the garden, and one was lost in a recent storm. They're going to replace it with a sculpture, which'll be made by students in their art lessons.

A slightly more unusual idea I came across is what they've done at Tower Road School. They've built a beach in their playground! It looks like a fun place for students to hang out, but the main reason it was put there was to encourage them to exercise. Students can try new activities that work better on sand than on the field. Around the beach area, there's a wall which has been covered in a brilliant painting designed by the art teacher and done by the students. It's of a ship, so it goes with the seaside theme. In front of the painting, there's a huge rock in the sand, surrounded by shells. It all looks amazing.

Another great idea I found was for an outdoor theatre. The outdoor stage at Low Beck School is built into a slope in the school grounds so audiences look down onto the stage. It was quite a complex project, but the school got loads of help from parents. The theatre was designed by two architects who were parents at the school, and built by a construction firm owned by parents. According to the school's website, it's got a stunning rural setting, so from every seat in the audience there are views of hills – they're all around the school, apparently. The town's busy streets are almost completely hidden from view because of the design of the theatre. In the summer, not only do they use the theatre for plays put on by the students, but they have concerts there too. It sounds an amazing place.

FURTHER PRACTICE

Put students into small groups to make a plan to improve the outdoor areas in their school. Give them time to brainstorm their ideas and prepare a short presentation for the rest of the class. When each presentation has been heard, the class can hold a vote to choose the most popular proposal.

Grammar

Conditionals

Before or after the lesson refer students to the QR codes to access *Grammar on the Move*.

1 If necessary, students can refer to the Grammar reference on page 87 before doing these exercises, or they could use it to check their answers once they have attempted to do the tasks. Go over the answers with the class.

Answers
1 'd/would spend
2 wouldn't have realised/discovered
3 'll/will have to
4 have to / must / should / need to

2 Encourage students to answer the questions individually, allowing enough time for the whole class to think about their answers before opening a class feedback session.

Answers
a 2   b 3   c 1   d 4

3 Point out that these examples show conditional sentences which use alternative expressions to *if*. Remind students that all these expressions are followed by the present tense even when we are talking about the future. Students complete the task before class feedback.

Answers
1 in case
2 unless
3 providing/provided (that); as/so long as

4 Allow time for students to do the task on their own before checking their answers with a partner. Check answers as a class.

Answers
1 in case
2 if
3 so long as
4 unless

Reading and Use of English

Part 1

Vocabulary – Phrasal verbs

1 Go over the instructions and allow time for students to find the verbs in the texts on page 39. When they have completed the list, encourage them to work with a partner to try to explain the meaning of each verb, using the context around them in the texts. Check answers as a class, eliciting the meaning of each verb.

Answers
Text A: miss out on; join in
Text B: help out
Text C: put on; pick up
Text D: make up for

2 Read through the exam tip and explain that this task gives students practice in the type of careful reading they need to do in Reading and Use of English Part 1. Students do the task on their own before checking answers with a partner. Go over the answers with the class.

> **Answers**
> 1 b   2 a   3 a   4 b   5 b   6 a

☑ Exam task

Remind students to read the title and the whole text for gist before thinking about the missing words. Set a time limit of around seven or eight minutes for students to complete the task on their own under exam conditions. Check answers as a class. If time allows, ask students to put some of the incorrect answer options into sentences or phrases to explain the meanings and use.

> **Exam task answers**
> 1 C   2 D   3 C   4 B   5 A   6 B   7 A   8 C

> **FURTHER PRACTICE**
>
> If time allows, put students into small groups to discuss the following: *Imagine you have been asked to plan a project to develop within your local community. What type of project would you implement? Who would benefit from it? Why does your community need this type of project?* Each group can give a brief presentation of their project to the rest of the class.

Part 4

3 Elicit anything students remember about Reading and Use of English Part 4. If necessary, allow them time to refer back to Unit 3 page 29. Read through the instructions and give students time to read through the two examples. Elicit answers from the class.

> **Answer**
> Example 1

4 Explain that students will now have some practice in looking at the type of vocabulary changes they should be able to make in this part of the exam. Students match the phrases on their own before checking answers with a partner.

> **Answers**
> 1 c   2 d   3 a   4 f   5 g   6 b   7 e

5 Remind students they will often have to change the grammar of the second sentence as well as the vocabulary. Allow time for the class to complete the exercise individually before checking answers as a class. Point out that in the exam there are two possible marks for each sentence so if they get the vocabulary correct but the grammar incorrect, they could still get one mark. It is important to encourage students to attempt to answer all the questions even if they are not certain of the answer.

> **Answers**
> 1 gets on well
> 2 had a disagreement
> 3 have participated
> 4 will go ahead
> 5 catching up with
> 6 are looking forward to moving
> 7 came across

☑ Exam task

Go over the exam tip with the class. Encourage them to read the instructions and remember not to change the form of the word given and not to use too many words. When they check their answers, they should ask themselves whether they have included all the information that was in the original sentence. In the exam, students should spend approximately 15 minutes doing this exercise, including time for checking their answers carefully. Students can work through the task in pairs or individually before class feedback.

> **Exam task answers**
> 1 wouldn't have | gone/come/travelled
> 2 are put | on
> 3 so/as long as | Sam is/'s
> 4 miss out on | seeing
> 5 has (got) many | interactive
> 6 was awarded | to

Speaking

Vocabulary – School subjects

> **STARTER**
> With books closed, lead a brief brainstorm to elicit the names of the subjects students study at school and any other subjects that are studied in other schools.

1 Open books and ask students to tick the subjects they study.

2 Encourage students to give reasons for their preferences using the expressions listed and adding any other details and explanations.

Part 1

3 Give students a minute to match the questions and answers. Then put them in pairs to ask and answer the questions using their own ideas, remembering to add reasons or explanations for their answers. Remind students that in Speaking Part 1 they will be asked questions about their everyday lives, interests and future plans. They are not expected to talk to their partner in this part of the exam. Allow students a few minutes to do the task.

Refer students to the Speaking bank on page 108 for further information if needed.

> **Answers**
> 1 C 2 B 3 D 4 A

> **FURTHER PRACTICE**
>
> Ask students to write two or three more questions under each of the two headings (*Ambitions and achievements* and *Education*). Then, in pairs they can ask and answer their questions, remembering to give extended answers.

Part 2

4 Elicit anything students remember about Speaking Part 2. If necessary, ask them how long they have to speak for (one minute), what they have to do (compare two photographs and answer a question about them), what they do after their partner finishes speaking (answer a short question about their partner's photographs, speaking for up to 30 seconds).

Go over the exam tip with the class and point out that students should use the language listed in the task if they are not sure of a word, or what is happening in the photos. Sometimes students find it difficult to keep speaking for a whole minute so they need to practise doing this and focus on answering the question rather than giving a detailed description of the photos.

✓ Exam task

Before students do the exam task in pairs, point out that here the students are asked to discuss the follow-up questions with their partner, whereas in the exam they will answer this question on their own. Make sure the listening student times the interaction so that students can get used to the feeling of speaking for one minute.

When students have finished, hold a brief class feedback session to discuss what students found most challenging about the task and what they think their partner did well.

Refer students to the Speaking bank on page 110 for further information if needed.

Writing

Part 2 article

> **STARTER**
>
> Introduce the topic by asking students where they might read an article. If possible, elicit: *magazines*, *newspapers* and *websites*. Hold a brief class discussion to find out what type of articles students read, how often they read articles and what topics they would like to read about and why.

1 Explain that the article in Writing Part 2 will usually be for an English-language magazine or website for teenagers so the style will be quite informal and lively. Read through the question with the students and allow them a few minutes to choose their answers. When going over answers with the class ask students to justify their ideas.

> **Answers**
> Tick: 1, 3, 5 and 6

2 Read the task with the class and ask some questions to check understanding, for example, *Where will the article be published? What should you include in it? How long is it?* Allow time for students to read the model answer, without worrying about the gaps for now, and highlight in different colours examples of the strategies in Ex 1. Students discuss their answers with a partner before class feedback.

> **Answers**
> 1 clear points – throughout article
> 3 interesting ending – last sentence
> 5 amusing comments – *it's not hard for me to choose which one was best; my friend Jordi kept quiet, which is extremely unusual; I think I learnt more that day than in a month at school!*
> 6 emotional responses – *We all felt really calm afterwards; I'll always remember that trip*

3 Remind students that the word count is important in the exam. If they write too much it may mean they are including irrelevant information or detail, and if they write too little they may not have answered all parts of the question. Ask students to suggest which sentence could be cut from the article they have just read. Discuss answers with the class.

4 Draw attention to the gaps in the article and point out that students were able to understand the message without these words as they are all linking words and expressions which help the organisation of the text but which do not add meaning. Remind students that it is important to use these words so that the writing is logical and easy to read. Allow a few minutes for students to do the task and then check their answers with a partner.

Answers
1 most importantly
2 also
3 Even
4 For instance
5 In fact

5 Put students into pairs to think about how the beginning and ending of this article could be different. Students may choose to use the strategies in Ex 1, such as starting with an amusing comment, or talking about an emotional reaction, and they should remember to finish in an interesting way. Ask one or two pairs to read their ideas out to the class for feedback.

☑ Exam task

Remind students how important it is to make a plan before they start writing, and to include all the points listed in the question. Students can brainstorm ideas and useful vocabulary with a partner at the planning stage but they should write their articles on their own. When giving feedback remember to comment on the points practised here (word count, linking expressions and organisation, the four strategies for keeping the reader's attention in Ex 1) as well as the grammar and vocabulary they use.

Refer students to the Writing bank on page 102 for further information if needed.

Model answer
Like most people, I rely heavily on the internet as a source of information. If I need to know anything, I immediately search for it on my smartwatch. But probably the best thing I've learnt on the internet is how to play the guitar.
I was given an acoustic guitar by my older brother about three years ago. He's a brilliant player, and had bought himself a better one. I was delighted, but couldn't play a note on it. After I pestered him and pestered him (typical little brother!), he taught me the chords for a few songs, but then got fed up and told me to learn from the internet, like he'd done. So I found an app which took me from the basics to a more advanced level at my own pace. One of the great things about it was being able to choose the kind of music I wanted to learn. I also had a few virtual lessons with teachers, which was really helpful and made me feel more confident in my ability.
So thanks, internet! You've given me a skill that brings me happiness every day.

6 Our planet

UNIT OBJECTIVES

TOPICS: environment and weather, wildlife

GRAMMAR: countable and uncountable nouns, articles, *so* and *such*, *too* and *enough*

VOCABULARY: climate, environmental problems, animals

READING AND USE OF ENGLISH PART 2: open cloze

PART 6: gapped text

WRITING PART 2: review

LISTENING PART 4: multiple-choice questions and long recording

SPEAKING PART 3: agreeing, disagreeing, making a comment or suggestion

PART 4: discussing ways of helping the environment

Listening

STARTER
Introduce the topic by writing *carbon footprint* next to an outline of a footprint on the board. Elicit the meaning of this and then ask students to suggest examples of activities and actions which increase or decrease a carbon footprint. Help students with vocabulary as needed.

1 Put students into pairs to match the pictures with the words in the box. Move round the class and provide help with vocabulary, if needed. Elicit feedback from a few different pairs.

> **Answers**
> a doing the laundry (washing machine)
> b heating and cooling systems (radiator)
> c electricity (lightning)
> d fossil fuels (petrol pump)
> e transport (van)
> f meat-based diets (bull)
> g waste (bin bag)
> h single-use plastic (plastic bottle)

2 Give students a minute or two to read through the text before they complete the gaps on their own. Ask them to check their answers with a partner before class feedback.

> **Answers**
> 1 carbon footprint   2 greenhouse gas   3 global warming
> 4 climate change   5 carbon emissions

3 Give pairs plenty of time to discuss their answers, encouraging them to say why each option is more or less environmentally friendly before matching the pictures with the ideas. When going through the answers note any new vocabulary on the board so that they can use it in Ex 4, for example, *renewable energy sources, eco-friendly, green energy*, etc.

> **Answers**
> 1 eating a vegan diet – lettuce leaves
> 2 electric cars – car with plug
> 3 drying clothes on a washing line – T-shirt on washing line
> 4 wind power – wind turbine
> 5 solar panels – sun and solar panels
> 6 recyclable plastic – plastic bag with recycle symbol
> 7 taking the train – train
> 8 saving energy – energy-saving light bulb

4 Allow two or three minutes for pairs to discuss their answers. Encourage them to use some of the vocabulary from the previous exercises. Elicit some answers from around the class to compare ideas.

Part 4

5 🔊 **15** Elicit or remind students of the format of Listening Part 4 (a longer recording with seven three-option multiple-choice questions) before reading through the task with the class, checking understanding. If necessary, explain that underlining the words in the questions which introduce the topic students are listening for can help to focus on the important information so that they know exactly what they are listening for. Play the recording, encouraging students to underline the topic words in the questions. Check answers as a class.

> **Answers**
> 1 What does the speaker say about <u>working out your carbon footprint</u>?
> 2 The speaker thinks that eating <u>organic food</u> …
> 3 Regarding <u>eating meat</u>, what does the speaker recommend?

> **Audio script Track 15**
>
> Working out your own carbon footprint is not easy because you're usually a consumer at the end of a long process. Take, for example, the carbon footprint of the food you eat. You have to consider the machinery and resources it uses to grow, harvest, package and transport it to the shops where you buy it. And more carbon is released when you cook it, of course.
>
> But simply by purchasing produce from local sources, it's possible to reduce your food's carbon footprint. Plus, if you choose to buy organic, then no chemicals will be used in its production, thereby reducing resources used further, thus lowering the overall carbon footprint. The type of foods you eat is also important, since vegetarian and vegan diets have much smaller carbon footprints than diets based on meat or other animal products – even going one or two days a week without meat can make a real difference. Finally, using electricity generated by renewable resources to cook your food can really help to bring that carbon footprint right down.

6 Photocopy the audio script so that the whole class can see it. Point out that the answers are always in the same order as the questions. Then show students that having identified the topic words before listening gives them a signal in the text that the answer is about to be given in each case. Allow students a few minutes to identify the answer to each question.

> **Answers**
> 1 It's not easy to do because you're a consumer at the end of a long process.
> 2 … can help reduce your carbon footprint as no chemicals are used in its production.
> 3 Cutting out meat one or two days a week.

7 🔊 **16** Read through the first exam tip with the class and remind students that identifying the topic words in the questions can provide a signal to help them focus carefully when they are about to hear the answers. Students compare answers with a partner before class feedback.

> **Answers**
> 1 inspired
> 2 survey
> 3 solar panels
> 4 tree planting
> 5 recycling improved
> 6 opinion, recycling
> 7 aim, Environment Exhibition

☑ Exam task

Refer students to the second exam tip which encourages students to keep listening to the whole recording without worrying too much if they miss an answer the first time they listen. They should at least be able to understand when to listen carefully for any answers they miss on the first listening when the recording is repeated.

Allow students some time to read through the answer options before they listen to the recording again to check and complete their answers.

> **Exam task answers**
> 1 B   2 C   3 C   4 B   5 B   6 B   7 A

Audio script Track 16

You will hear an interview with a boy called Thomas who is talking about the environment club he started at his school. For questions 1–7, choose the best answer (A, B or C).

Interviewer: On tonight's programme about local issues, I'm talking to 16-year-old student Thomas Townsend, who goes to Oldwood School. He's going to tell us about the environment club he started at his school. So Thomas, I understand you set up the club two years ago, after you invited a visitor to your school?

Thomas: That's right. I'd seen a video online about global warming – that famous one made by Al Gore, the American politician. It made me want to do something, but I wasn't sure what, so I emailed Rich Gray, an ecologist who runs an environment group. He came

and gave a really inspiring talk to the whole school, telling us about everything from getting support from big businesses, to picking up rubbish around school.

Interviewer: Right, so what action have you taken at the school so far?

Thomas: Well, after I formed the club with students in my year, we wanted to focus on reducing the school's carbon footprint. So first, we surveyed how students and staff travelled to school. We found that while most students walked, many teachers came by car. They were a bit embarrassed when we pointed this out to them! So they decided to car share more – instead of driving to school individually, they take it in turns to give each other lifts so the numbers driving in have halved.

Interviewer: That's great. And I believe you raised some money for solar panels to power the school, too?

Thomas: We did. My friend's family is really into the environment, and their farm's completely solar powered, so they advised us on the best panels for the school. Unbelievably, it only took us a term to raise enough money to get some. They're just powering the school kitchen and restaurant right now, but we aim to get more next year because they've been such a success.

Interviewer: Excellent. How else did you go about reducing the carbon footprint of the school?

Thomas: We planted trees, which will absorb carbon dioxide from the air.

Interviewer: Right – but trees take up lots of space. Do you now have less room for other outdoor activities like sports?

Thomas: Er … some parents were worried about that, and campaigned against the tree planting, so we agreed to plant eight rather than the 12 we'd originally decided on. That was a shame, because I'm sure the extra four wouldn't have made much difference. Anyway, the ones we put in are great.

Interviewer: Well done. I understand you and your friends have also improved recycling at the school?

Thomas: Yes, that's an ongoing campaign. One of the first things our environment club did was to look at what students were throwing away in the bins around school.

Interviewer: Not a pleasant job!

Thomas: Horrible! But worth doing because we found that 70% of the rubbish could have been recycled.

Interviewer: Wow!

Thomas: So we organised new recycling bins for the school: separate ones for plastic, paper and cardboard, and metal. When we checked most recently, in the general waste bins only 25% of the rubbish put in them could have been recycled, which is pretty good.

Interviewer: That's impressive.

Thomas: But of course, although recycling's great, what's better is cutting the total amount of stuff we use in the first place – a much more effective way of reducing our carbon footprint, as less energy is used to produce things. For instance, our school and plenty of others have installed more water fountains – taps where students can fill their own bottles rather than drinking from single-use plastic bottles and then recycling them.

Interviewer: Yes, I see. So, what's next for the environment club, Thomas?

Thomas: We're organising an Environment Exhibition.

Interviewer: Right, and what does that involve exactly?

Thomas:	So, there are about 15 active members of the environment club, and we've all contributed to the projects we've worked on, but now we're feeling a bit stuck. <u>We'd really welcome some inspiration from outside the club.</u> So we're going to create a display showing what's been achieved so far, and <u>encourage people to make suggestions as to what we do next.</u>
Interviewer:	Fantastic! Good luck with that, Thomas.

8 Give pairs a copy of the script without underlining (see below) and allow them time to read and underline the sections of the text which give the answers. They could also highlight the parts which show that the other answers are incorrect. Hold a brief feedback session to discuss answers.

> **Answers**
> See underlining in audio script above for answers.

Audio script Track 16

Interviewer:	On tonight's programme about local issues, I'm talking to 16-year-old student Thomas Townsend, who goes to Oldwood School. He's going to tell us about the environment club he started at his school. So Thomas, I understand you set up the club two years ago, after you invited a visitor to your school?
Thomas:	That's right. I'd seen a video online about global warming – that famous one made by Al Gore, the American politician. It made me want to do something, but I wasn't sure what, so I emailed Rich Gray, an ecologist who runs an environment group. He came and gave a really inspiring talk to the whole school, telling us about everything from getting support from big businesses, to picking up rubbish around school.
Interviewer:	Right, so what action have you taken at the school so far?
Thomas:	Well, after I formed the club with students in my year, we wanted to focus on reducing the school's carbon footprint. So first, we surveyed how students and staff travelled to school. We found that while most students walked, many teachers came by car. They were a bit embarrassed when we pointed this out to them! So they decided to car share more – instead of driving to school individually, they take it in turns to give each other lifts so the numbers driving in have halved.
Interviewer:	That's great. And I believe you raised some money for solar panels to power the school, too?
Thomas:	We did. My friend's family is really into the environment, and their farm's completely solar powered, so they advised us on the best panels for the school. Unbelievably, it only took us a term to raise enough money to get some. They're just powering the school kitchen and restaurant right now, but we aim to get more next year because they've been such a success.
Interviewer:	Excellent. How else did you go about reducing the carbon footprint of the school?
Thomas:	We planted trees, which will absorb carbon dioxide from the air.
Interviewer:	Right – but trees take up lots of space. Do you now have less room for other outdoor activities like sports?
Thomas:	Er … some parents were worried about that, and campaigned against the tree planting, so we agreed to plant eight rather than the 12 we'd originally decided on. That was a shame, because I'm sure the extra four

	wouldn't have made much difference. Anyway, the ones we put in are great.
Interviewer:	Well done. I understand you and your friends have also improved recycling at the school?
Thomas:	Yes, that's an ongoing campaign. One of the first things our environment club did was to look at what students were throwing away in the bins around school.
Interviewer:	Not a pleasant job!
Thomas:	Horrible! But worth doing because we found that 70% of the rubbish could have been recycled.
Interviewer:	Wow!
Thomas:	So we organised new recycling bins for the school: separate ones for plastic, paper and cardboard, and metal. When we checked most recently, in the general waste bins only 25% of the rubbish put in them could have been recycled, which is pretty good.
Interviewer:	That's impressive.
Thomas:	But of course, although recycling's great, what's better is cutting the total amount of stuff we use in the first place – a much more effective way of reducing our carbon footprint, as less energy is used to produce things. For instance, our school and plenty of others have installed more water fountains – taps where students can fill their own bottles rather than drinking from single-use plastic bottles and then recycling them.
Interviewer:	Yes, I see. So, what's next for the environment club, Thomas?
Thomas:	We're organising an Environment Exhibition at school.
Interviewer:	Right, and what does that involve exactly?
Thomas:	So, there are about 15 active members of the environment club, and we've all contributed to the projects we've worked on, but now we're feeling a bit stuck. We'd really welcome some inspiration from outside the club. So we're going to create a display showing what's been achieved so far, and encourage people to make suggestions as to what we do next.
Interviewer:	Fantastic! Good luck with that, Thomas.

FURTHER PRACTICE
Students work in small groups to discuss any similar initiatives which they have participated in at their school or that they have heard about in other schools.

Speaking

Part 3

STARTER
With books closed, elicit suggestions from around the class for ideas of how students can improve or protect the environment at school, before opening books and checking to see whether there are any other ideas in the spidergram that they did not mention.

1 Focus attention on the question and the spidergram and put students into pairs to make brief notes, not sentences, on their ideas. Remind students that the vocabulary from the audio script may be helpful. Move around the class to prompt and support as needed. Elicit some suggestions to compare ideas.

2 Allow a few minutes for students to complete the task on their own. When checking answers focus on the intonation of the expressions. Remind students that in the Speaking test they are assessed on various aspects of pronunciation, including intonation, and if they use these expressions without the appropriate intonation, they can sound quite unnatural and mechanical.

> **Answers**
> 1 I don't really think that's a good idea. (D)
> 2 Absolutely. (A)
> 3 We all know we shouldn't drop litter. (C)
> 4 We could tell everyone to turn off their computers at the end of the lesson. (S)
> 5 I don't think turning the heating down would go down well with students here. (C)
> 6 I'm with you on that. (A)
> 7 That's not what I think, I'm afraid. (D)
> 8 What about getting recycling bins in the canteen? (S)

☑ Exam task

Read the exam tip with the class, pointing out that in the exam they will have some time to read the question and the ideas before they are asked to start speaking. Then, they have two minutes to discuss the ideas together so they may not have time to talk about all of them. Remind them to use some of the questions suggested to include their partner in the discussion, as well as the expressions in Ex 2 to respond to what their partner says. Put students with a different partner to practise the exam task. Monitor as students are speaking and make a note of any common errors to go through with the whole class when they finish.

Refer students to the Speaking bank on page 114 for further Information if needed.

Part 4

☑ Exam task

In Speaking Part 4 students cannot read the questions, so it could be helpful to put students into groups of three with one student playing the role of the examiner and asking the questions while the other two students close their books and answer the questions with their partner. Explain that in Part 4 sometimes the examiner will ask each student their own question and sometimes they will ask the two students to discuss their answers to a question together.

Refer students to the Speaking bank on page 116 for further information if needed.

Writing

Part 2 review

> **STARTER**
> With books closed, elicit the names of some everyday objects that are made of plastic.

1 Open books and read through the instructions with the class. Draw attention to the words in the table and check understanding by asking students to give synonyms or to use the words in sentences. For example, re-use = use again, harm = damage, durable = able to last for a long time, and so on. Elicit one or two suggestions about the plastic bottle from around the class to demonstrate the activity before putting students into pairs to continue the discussion. Check answers by asking different pairs to tell the class their ideas.

> **Suggested answers**
> Bottle: Can be recycled but many aren't, and end up in the oceans, polluting the environment, harming marine wildlife. Alternative: use a more durable drinks bottle not made of plastic.
> Bag: breaks easily so single use, most are non-recyclable. Alternative: use a cotton or other fabric bag.
> Toothbrush is non-recyclable, and plastic is not biodegradable, so will end up polluting the oceans or in landfill. Alternative: one made of natural materials, e.g. bamboo which will biodegrade.

2 Elicit some general information about Writing Part 2 before asking what students remember about the characteristics of a review. If necessary, refer students to the Writing bank on page 100.

Draw attention to the exam task and allow a few minutes for students to read it and answer the question. Go over the answers with the class.

> **Answers**
> 1 information about what the shop sells
> 2 information about customer service at the shop
> 3 whether you would recommend the shop to other people your age

3 Read through the instructions with the class before putting students into pairs to read the model answer and then write a few sentences to add the missing information. Ask them to decide where the new section should be added. You could also ask them to split the text into clear paragraphs.

> **Answer**
> Customer service information is missing.

> **Sample answer**
> Customer service there is excellent. The shop's run by a married couple who have owned it for about 20 years. They both love books and they're really friendly and knowledgeable. They always tell you exactly where to find the book you're looking for if they've got it in stock. If they haven't, they will be happy to try and find a copy for you elsewhere and order it for you.

☑ Exam task

4 Allow students time to read the instructions and the exam task carefully. Then elicit the key information that their reviews must include (where you can get the product, why it is environmentally friendly, whether they would recommend it to a person of their age).

Encourage students to make notes of their ideas for each of the three content points. They should also try to think about some appropriate vocabulary and try to include some of the words in the box in Ex 1. They can do this preparation in pairs or individually.

Students write their reviews on their own in about 40 minutes. Remind them to leave time to check their work. Some students can read their reviews out to the class or you can take them in for correction.

> **Model answer**
> One environmentally-friendly thing I have is a drinks bottle. I was given it last year by my dad, who got it from a shop online. They are commonly available online and in many shops. I use this bottle every day. I fill it up in the morning, and take it to school with me, or wherever else I'm going that day. The reason that it is environmentally friendly is that it reduces plastic waste. It means I don't have to buy bottles of water made of single-use plastic, or use and throw away plastic cups. I highly recommend my drinks bottle. I have already had it for a year, and it's still in good condition. Another great thing about it is the way the water inside it stays cool. That's great in the summer. The only slight problem with it is that it isn't large enough when I'm doing sports on hot days. On those days, I have to take two bottles with me.

Reading and Use of English

STARTER
Lead a brief class brainstorm session to introduce the topic of wildlife by asking students to name any wild animals they know and then to say whether they live in the wild in their country or in other parts of the world.

1 Draw attention to the photos and give students a few minutes to identify and name the (parts of the) animals they can see. Check answers as a class.

> **Answers**
> A zebra   B owl   C wasp   D crocodile   E crab

2 Put students into pairs to ask and answer the questions. If necessary, they can use a dictionary to check any vocabulary. Go over the answers with the class, eliciting any other animals they can name for each category.

> **Answers**
> (there could be some debate on some of these)
> 1 eagle, owl, swan, wasp   2 owl, wolf, crocodile   3 worm
> 4 (some parts of some) eagles, wasp, zebra   5 crab   6 seal
> 7 crab, wasp   8 Students' own answers

Part 6

3 Elicit from the class what they remember about Reading and Use of English Part 6 before drawing attention to the task. If necessary, elicit one or two ideas for the first sentence to check understanding of the task before allowing pairs time to note down some suggestions for the other sentences. Go over the answers with the class,

focusing on the words which help with text cohesion, such as linkers showing contrast (*But*) or addition (*Plus*), pronouns (*This*), etc.

> **Suggested answers**
> 1 In winter, the sea is occasionally calm.
> 2 Survey results showed that teenagers ate much more healthily than adults.
> 3 At the school council, students voted in favour of creating a wildlife garden.
> 4 The park is full of beautiful flowers which visitors love to see.
> 5 You could do your conservation project on butterflies.
> 6 The wildlife group have raised money to construct a tunnel under the road.

4 Draw attention to the instructions and the title of the exam task, and ask students to predict what the text might be about. Accept all answers before allowing them a minute or two to read the text to check whether any of their predictions were accurate. Then ask students to scan the text to find the words in the list. Encourage them to use the context to match the words with the definitions. Students check answers with a partner before class feedback.

> **Answers**
> 1 h   2 g   3 f   4 a   5 d   6 c   7 e   8 b

✓ Exam task

Refer students to the exam tip and then allow them 10 to 15 minutes to complete the task on their own.

> **Exam task answers**
> 1 E   2 F   3 B   4 G   5 A   6 C

5 Put students into pairs to work through and discuss the questions, then elicit answers from around the class.

FURTHER PRACTICE
Encourage students to do some research to find out about a citizen science project they would like to participate in. In pairs, students give a short presentation to the class explaining the project and saying why they would like to get involved.

Grammar

Countable and uncountable nouns

Before or after the lesson refer students to the QR code to access *Grammar on the Move*.

Point out that the grammar focus in this unit is useful for Reading and Use of English Parts 1 and 2 as well as the Writing paper.

1 2 Go through the first two questions with the class and then give students a minute or two to find examples in the text to complete the table.

> **Answers**
> 1 Countable nouns can be singular or plural.
> 2 Uncountable nouns cannot be plural and take a singular verb.
> Possible answers:
> Countable: insect, expert, scientist
> Uncountable: species, equipment, science

Articles

Before or after the lesson refer students to the QR code to access *Grammar on the Move*.

3 Encourage students to complete the rules on their own before referring to the Grammar reference on page 90 to check their answers, if necessary.

> **Answers**
> 1 a; an   2 the   3 the   4 no article   5 no article   6 the

4 Refer students to the headings and elicit an example for each one before putting students into pairs to complete the task.

> **Answers**
> Oceans, seas and rivers: the Amazon, the Atlantic Ocean, the Thames
> Regions: the Far East, the north of England
> Countries (with the word *republic*, *kingdom*, *states*): the Czech Republic, the United Kingdom, the United States
> Deserts and mountain ranges: the Himalayas, the Sahara
> NB The following do not need *the* in front of them: California, Italy, Lake Como, London, South America

5 Students complete the task alone before checking answers with a partner. When going through the answers encourage students to explain their answers by referring to the rules in Ex 3.

> **Answers**
> 1 a; the   2 a; the   3 the; a   4 the; a   5 a; the

6 Give students a few minutes to do the task with a partner before checking answers as a class.

> **Answers**
> 1 –   2 the   3 the   4 –

So and such (a/an)

Before or after the lesson refer students to the QR code to access *Grammar on the Move*.

7 Students work through the task with a partner before class feedback.

> **Answers**
> 1 so   2 such   3 such   4 so   5 so   6 such

8 Encourage students to use the sentences in Ex 7 to complete the rules. Refer them to the Grammar reference on page 91 if necessary.

> **Answers**
> such; so

Too and enough

9 Students complete the sentence about the photo. After answers have been checked elicit some other example sentences using *too* or *enough* from the students about their classroom, school, home, etc. Refer students to the Grammar reference on page 91 as necessary.

> **Answers**
> big enough; too big

Reading and Use of English

Part 2

1 Elicit information and tips for Reading and Use of English Part 2 from the class. If necessary, refer them to Student's Book page 18 to remind themselves of the task. Explain that Ex 1 helps students to remember the typical focus of the questions in Part 2. Put students into pairs to complete the task before class feedback.

> **Answers**
> 1 d   2 h   3 g   4 i   5 a   6 c   7 b   8 f   9 e

2 Go over the example with the class, checking understanding. Then students read the rest of the text in the exam task and match the gaps with the list of focuses from Ex 1. Check answers as a class.

> **Answers**
> 0 superlative form   1 verb tense   2 linking phrase
> 3 pronoun   4 phrasal verb   5 preposition   6 pronoun
> 7 linking phrase   8 form of *there is/are*

✓ Exam task

Go over the exam tip, reminding students that in the exam they can write their answers on the question paper but they have to transfer them to the separate answer sheet before the end of the exam. This may be a good moment to remind students that in Reading and Use of English their spelling must be correct and they should make sure that their handwriting is clear. They should write their answers in capital letters on the answer sheet using a pencil.

Set a time limit of about ten minutes for students to complete the task on their own.

> **Exam task answers**
> 1 been   2 not   3 It   4 about   5 since   6 which   7 though
> 8 there

3 Students compare their answers with a partner before class feedback.

FURTHER PRACTICE

Put students into pairs to research another endangered animal and find out about any conservation programmes in place to protect it. They should write a short text using the exam task text as a model.

UNIT OBJECTIVES

TOPICS: buying and selling, people and feelings

GRAMMAR: verbs and expressions followed by *to* + infinitive or *-ing* form, reported speech

VOCABULARY: shopping, feelings

READING AND USE OF ENGLISH PART 4: key-word transformations

PART 5: multiple-choice questions

WRITING PART 2: letter and email, giving information, using linking words and phrases

LISTENING PART 3: listening for details and general understanding

SPEAKING PART 1: expressing likes and dislikes

PART 2: comparing different ways of shopping

Reading and Use of English

STARTER

Introduce the topic with books closed by writing *Buying and selling* on the board and asking students to brainstorm vocabulary they associate with these words. Encourage them to think about any recent experiences they have had of buying or selling things. Make a note of any useful or new words on the board for students to use when they answer the questions in the Student's Book.

1 Focus attention on the photos and elicit suggestions from around the class. Encourage students to justify their answers.

Answers
Photo A: selling, online, entrepreneur
Photo B: buying, in-store, consumer

2 Go over the first phrase with the class to demonstrate the task if necessary. Then allow time for students to complete the exercise on their own. Move round the class and provide help with vocabulary if needed. Elicit feedback from a few different students.

Answers

Who ...	The seller	The buyer
is trying to make a profit?	✓	
is making a living?	✓	
is using a debit card?		✓
is purchasing something?		✓
is earning an income?	✓	
is running a business?	✓	
is making a payment?		✓
gets stock from suppliers?	✓	
trades goods over the internet?	✓	
is at the counter?		✓
might be getting a bargain?		✓

3 If necessary, check understanding of the words in the box by eliciting an example of each one. Put students into pairs to discuss their answers to the questions. Elicit some answers from around the class to open into a brief discussion to compare opinions.

Part 5

4 Read through the exam tip with the class and explain that this exercise gives them practice in using this strategy. Allow time for students to complete the task, then ask them to compare their answers with a partner before class feedback.

Answers
1 b 2 d 3 a 4 f 5 c 6 e

5 Elicit any tips students remember about how to approach Reading and Use of English Part 5 and, if necessary, tell them that reading the title and the first paragraph (or the whole text) quickly for gist can help them predict the content, which in turn makes it easier to understand the text. Set a short time limit to encourage students to read for gist rather than detailed understanding before eliciting answers.

✓ Exam task

Encourage students to read the instructions before setting a time limit of around 10 to 15 minutes for them to complete the task. Check answers with the class, eliciting which part of the text provides the answer to each question.

FURTHER PRACTICE

Students work in small groups to discuss what type of entrepreneurial project they would like to be part of. They can create a basic 'business plan' for their idea, describing their target customers, what their app or website would look like and any other details, and then present it to the rest of the class.

Speaking

Part 1

STARTER

Elicit any information students remember about Speaking Part 1. Ask questions about timing (two minutes), and the type of questions they may be asked (personal questions about likes and dislikes, leisure time, future plans, etc.).

1 🔊 **17** Read the instructions with the class and check understanding before playing the recording. Check answers as a class.

Answers
Lara:
Like: art, painting, going to art galleries, skiing, beach
Dislike: mountains in summer, long walks, looking at the views
Jacob:
Like: watching rugby, English and geography
Dislike: playing rugby and other sports

Audio script Track 17

Examiner: What do you like doing in your free time, Lara?

Lara: I'm really into art, so I spend a lot of time painting and I enjoy going to art galleries. I attempt to draw or paint something new every day and one day I hope to be a successful artist.

Examiner: Jacob, do you like sports?

Jacob: I'm mad about rugby, of course, like everyone who comes from my town. I love going to see them when they play at home.

Examiner: And do you play any sports?

Jacob: I'm not very keen on playing rugby myself. I prefer to watch it. And I don't really like playing other sports very much either.

Examiner: Lara, what do you like to do when you're on holiday?

Lara: I live near the sea so we usually go to the mountains for holidays. I'm very keen on skiing. I love to spend time out on the snow. I first learnt when I was four years old, so I'm quite good at it now.

Examiner: What about summer holidays?

Lara: I'm not that interested in going to the mountains in the summer. I can't bear going for long walks and looking at the views. I suppose it's because my parents made me do it when I was little. I prefer being at the beach.

Examiner: What's your favourite subject at school, Jacob?

Jacob: Well, history is OK but it's not my favourite. English and geography are what I enjoy most. I don't mind doing science but I'm not very good at the practical stuff – the experiments. I'd prefer to study things like the history of science. I want to study history at university. I'd like to be a history teacher one day.

2 Give students time to read through the phrases and complete any they think they remember before playing the recording again for students to check and complete their answers. When going over the answers highlight the prepositions which are often part of the phrases.

Answers
1 I'm really into art.
2 I enjoy going to art galleries.
3 I'm mad about rugby, of course.
4 I love going to see them.
5 I'm very keen on skiing.
6 English and geography are what I enjoy most.
7 I'm not very keen on playing rugby myself.
8 I don't really like playing other sports very much.
9 I'm not that interested in going to the mountains in the summer.
10 I can't bear going for long walks.
11 Well, history is OK but it's not my favourite.
12 I don't mind doing science.

✅ Exam task

Read the exam tip with the class and point out that the questions in brackets can be used if the answer to the main question is too short. Put students into pairs to ask and answer the questions. Encourage them to listen carefully to their partner's answers and give them feedback on whether they answered the question correctly with reasons and examples, whether they used any good vocabulary and whether they were able to answer immediately without too much hesitation.

Refer students to the Speaking bank on page 108 for further information if needed.

Part 2

3 Refer students to the photos and lead a brief class discussion to answer the question.

4 🔊 **18** Elicit from the class what is required in Speaking Part 2 before reading the instructions and the suggested advantages and disadvantages. Then play the recording. Students check their answers with a partner before class feedback.

Answers
He talks about photos C and D.
Advantages: compare prices, convenient, lots of choice, more fun, you can try clothes on
Disadvantages: can't try things on, not much for teenagers, quite traditional, wait for the post

5 Read through the first exam tip with the class and point out that Adam used some expressions to give himself a few seconds to think about his answers. Play the recording again and ask students to complete the expressions. Elicit answers from around the class, focusing on accurate intonation and stress when students say the phrases.

> **Answers**
> 1 Mmm, let me see ...
> 2 Let me think for a moment ...
> 3 Not everyone would agree but I think ...

6 Put students into pairs to brainstorm some ideas together before eliciting suggestions from around the class.

7 Students work with a different partner to list some ideas for the other two photographs. Offer support with vocabulary as needed while students are working.

☑ Exam task

Read through the second exam tip with the class and, if necessary, elicit exactly what students need to do in Speaking Part 2. Ask them questions about timing (they should speak about the photos for one minute and have up to 30 seconds to answer a question about their partner's pictures) and what they have to talk about (similarities and differences between the photographs as well as answering the question at the top of the page).

Read through the connecting phrases with the class before putting them into pairs to complete the exam task. The listening student should time their partner. When students have finished the task, ask each one to answer the question *Which of these activities would you prefer to do?* about the two photos their partner discussed, reminding them to give reasons for their opinions.

Refer students to the Speaking bank on page 110 for further information if needed.

Grammar

Verbs and expressions followed by *to* + infinitive or *-ing* form

Before or after the lesson refer students to the QR code to access *Grammar on the Move*.

1 Put students into pairs to do the task. Encourage them to put the verbs and expressions into phrases and listen to which verb form 'sounds better'. Students may be surprised to learn that they can do some exercises in this way as they have frequently heard the expressions used. Go over the answers with the class, eliciting phrases. Refer students to the Grammar reference on page 91 if necessary.

> **Answers**
> *to* + infinitive: attempt, hope, want, would like, would prefer
> *-ing* form: don't mind, enjoy, be interested in, be keen on, suggest (Q4), dream of (Q7)
> either *to* + infinitive or *-ing* form: can't bear, like, love, prefer

2 Students complete the exercise on their own before checking answers with a partner. Go through the answers with the class and remind students to complete the headings in Ex 1.

> **Answers**
> 1 going   2 meet   3 to come   4 walking   5 to go   6 to go
> 7 living   8 to visit   9 to buy   10 playing

Reported speech

Before or after the lesson refer students to the QR code to access *Grammar on the Move*.

3 Students can read the Grammar reference on page 92 before or after doing the exercise with a partner. Check answers as a class.

> **Answers**
> 1 worked   2 was having   3 'd/had never ridden
> 4 'd/had got; 'd/had eaten   5 'd/would ring; got
> 6 could; couldn't

4 Draw attention to the task and let students write their own answers as they think about the question. Allow students time to discuss their answers with a partner before class feedback.

> **Answers**
> The girl's mum asked her how she was.
> The girl's mum asked (her) if she wanted to go shopping.
> (We use *come* when we ask someone to join us in doing something but, when we report the sentence, *come* changes to *go*.)
> We use *if* when we report a *yes/no* question.

5 Students can do the task on their own or with a partner before class feedback.

Answers

1 why he was so sad.
2 what she was listening to.
3 if his team had won.
4 if there were any leftovers.
5 if she had seen his wallet.
6 if he would be home late.

6 Explain to students that this exercise focuses on verb patterns, rather than the differences in meanings of the verbs. If necessary, go through the first two verbs with the class explaining that *advised* fits but *agreed* doesn't fit in the sentence as *agree* is not followed by the object (*her*). Students complete the exercise on their own before checking answers as a class.

Answers

The verbs which fit the gap are: advised, asked, encouraged, persuaded, reminded, told, warned
The verbs which don't fit the gap are: agreed, explained, mentioned, said
Agree isn't followed directly by an object like *her*, and *said, explained* and *mentioned* would be followed by *to her*.

7 Students complete the exercise using their answers to Ex 6 to check if needed. Go over the answers as a class, asking students to make a sentence using the incorrect option, if time allows.

Answers

1 told   2 agreed   3 warned   4 mention

8 Encourage students to do the exercise on their own or with a partner before checking answers as a class.

Answers

1 said   2 told   3 asked   4 told them   5 told   6 asked
7 told   8 asked

Reading and Use of English

Part 4

STARTER
Elicit anything students remember about Reading and Use of English Part 4. Use questions to elicit some information if necessary. For example, *How many words do you have to use in your answer?* (between two and five), *What must you include?* (the word given, without changing it), and remind students that contractions count as two words (e.g. they're = they are). Draw attention to the exam task if necessary.

1 Explain that this exercise gives students practice in the type of paraphrasing they will need to use in this part of the exam. Students do the exercise on their own or with a partner before class feedback.

Answers

1 g   2 e   3 j   4 a   5 c   6 i   7 b   8 f   9 d   10 h

✓ Exam task

Before students do the task, ask them to read the instructions carefully and underline the three points they need to remember, then elicit *so that it has a similar meaning, using the word given, do not change the word, and use between two and five words.* It is important that students understand that their answer must fulfil all these points in order to be correct. Read the exam tip with the class and use the example sentence to illustrate that students would get one mark if they wrote *such a* and the second mark if they wrote *long film.* Finally, give students ten minutes to complete the task under exam conditions, i.e. on their own without conferring. Check answers as a class.

Exam task answers

1 warned me | not to
2 the most | successful
3 wished they | 'd/had gone/been
4 than | going for/with
5 if/whether | I'd/had seen
6 reminded Ben | to

Listening

STARTER
With books closed, brainstorm adjectives to describe feelings. If necessary, prompt students with questions about situations, e.g. *How do you feel if the bus is late / your teacher gives you a lot of homework / your favourite team wins a match?* Help with spelling and pronunciation as needed.

1 Draw attention to the photos and the list of adjectives. Elicit or explain the meaning of any unknown words. Then put students into pairs to discuss their answers to the questions. Elicit answers from the class.

Answers

A astonished   B irritated   C amused

2 Pair students with a different partner to discuss their answers to the question. Encourage the listening partner to ask questions to elicit more detail about each situation. Ask some pairs to tell the class about their experiences.

3 Give students time to do the task on their own before checking answers with a partner. Then check answers as a class.

Answers

1 c   2 d   3 a   4 b

4 🔊 **19** Read the instructions with the class and explain that students have to infer the type of person each friend is from the information given on the recording, rather than listening for the adjectives listed in the answers. This is the same strategy they will have to use in the exam task. Play the recording twice if necessary to allow students to check their answers.

> **Answers**
> 1 A   2 C   3 C

> **Audio script Track 19**
> The first friend I want to talk about is Tobias. He is lovely to spend time with because he never seems to be stressed about anything, so he makes you feel relaxed too.
>
> My second friend is Gregor. He's great but in a different way from Tobias. I love the way he gets passionate about things he cares about, like equal rights. He helps me understand important issues.
>
> And last but not least, Mickey. At first, I didn't particularly like him because he's so serious – you hardly ever see him laugh! But he's really kind – he's a great guy.

Part 3

☑ Exam task

🔊 **20** Read through the instructions and the exam tip with the class. Remind students that in the exam they will have 30 seconds to read through the question and answer options before they listen. They should use this time to think about other ways of expressing the meaning of each option. Ask students to do the task under exam conditions, i.e. without conferring, and listening to the recording twice, before checking answers as a class.

> **Exam task answers**
> 1 F   2 E   3 D   4 A   5 C

> **Audio script Track 20**
> *You will hear five short extracts in which teenagers are talking about how an influencer on social media made them feel.*
>
> *For questions 1–5, choose from the list (A–H) how each speaker felt. Use the letters only once. There are three extra letters which you do not need to use.*
>
> Speaker 1:   I used to follow Jackson Zee, who started off as a fashion influencer, but then got into green issues. I only followed him for a few months because every day he was telling his followers something else that we should be doing to save the planet. It seemed like my efforts to be green were never enough, which started to bother me, as I believe protecting the environment is important. Occasionally, thinking about his posts even kept me awake at night. So I stopped following him and looked for someone more relaxing to follow!
>
> Speaker 2:   This one influencer I used to follow wouldn't post stuff very often, but when she did, it was obvious that she just wanted to shock people so they'd respond to her. They were usually about crazy things she said she'd done – but actually I'm pretty sure she didn't do half of the things she claimed. Sometimes she told people to go and do things that she thought were funny. She got loads of likes, loads of shares, but it got on my nerves after a while, which is why I don't follow her any more.
>
> Speaker 3:   Last summer, the singer Fly Nixon did some public sessions on a social media app, but they weren't her usual fun dance music events, they were to help people who tend to worry a lot. Apparently, she's like that herself. She was showing people some breathing exercises that she does every day to help stop her getting stressed. She also explains ways of thinking positively about things. After I'd watched these sessions, I noticed I was more relaxed, and thousands of people all round the world said the same thing in the comments.
>
> Speaker 4:   One influencer I followed was Davina Brooks. She was brilliant at what she did, which was mostly promoting fashion clothing for teenagers my age. She made it seem like what she thought was the only opinion that mattered, and unfortunately, I started to believe her. So much so that I felt I needed to check my phone all the time so I could see what she was saying – I didn't want to miss anything. Then one day I lost my phone, and after an initial mad panic, I realised I didn't need someone else to tell me what I thought!
>
> Speaker 5:   Richie Jones was a social media star who focused on food and cooking. Lots of my friends were talking about him, and how amazing he was, so I started following him. I wasn't disappointed, he was great – it's a real shame he's stopped doing his videos to focus on TV work. He was so good at making it seem like eating healthily wasn't boring and difficult; it could actually be fun. So I'd say it's down to him that I've improved my diet. I learnt a few easy recipes from him, which I often make now for my family.

> **FURTHER PRACTICE**
> Put students into small groups to discuss their own experiences and feelings, both positive and negative, around influencers or other famous people on social media.

Writing

Part 2 email / letter

1 When introducing the task, remind students that linking words and phrases are important in every piece of writing they do. Go over the instructions with the class and put students into pairs to complete the exercise. When checking answers, point out the structure of the email/letter, highlighting the opening and closing salutations and the organisation into paragraphs.

> **Answers**
> 1 Apart from the fact that
> 2 One of the main ones
> 3 managed to
> 4 Another reason
> 5 not because
> 6 That said
> 7 Yet
> 8 even

2 Allow students time to reread the letter and underline the adjectives used to describe Sheku Kanneh Mason's personality. Check answers as a class.

> **Answers**
> strong, determined, genuine, passionate, shy

3 Give students a few minutes to decide which famous person they would like to describe before putting them into pairs to discuss their answers to the questions. Move around the room offering support with vocabulary as needed.

4 Go over the list of points to remember with the class, eliciting different examples of ways to start and end the letter. Then give students time to write their letters. They can exchange their letter with a partner for peer feedback using the checklist.

5 Put students into pairs with a new partner to discuss their answers to the questions. Encourage them to make notes.

☑ Exam task

Give students time to read the instructions and the email from Andrew. Then elicit information students know about Writing Part 2. If necessary, ask them about timing (in the exam they have 40 minutes), number of words (140–190), style (this is an email to a friend so they should use informal language) and organisation (paragraphs and linking words and phrases). Remind students to leave time to check spelling and grammar after they finish writing. Students can write their email individually in class or at home. Refer to the Writing bank on page 98 for further information if needed.

> **Model answers**
> 1
> Dear Andrew,
> You asked me to write and tell you about the person I admire most in my family. It's definitely my mother.
> She always manages to be cheerful, and she's very patient with my little brothers and me. She never gets discouraged, even when we do badly at school, and somehow she gets us organised so we can sort things out for ourselves. She's thoughtful too, so we always get birthday presents that we really like, and at weekends we have fun with her and Dad, just going to the beach near us, or having friends round.
> Mum has a job. She's a manager in the local supermarket, so she works hard. Despite having very little time for herself while we were young, she's done very well, and she got promoted quickly.
> As you can see, I'm lucky to have a mum like this, and my brothers think so too.
> I hope that answers your question.
> Best wishes
> Tim

2
Dear Julia,
You wanted me to write and tell you about a student in my college that I admire. I'm not going to tell you about someone who is the cleverest person in the school, or the best at sport, or even the best looking.
I'm going to tell you about Robbie, who comes to school every day in his wheelchair. I've known him since he was at primary school, and he has been in his chair for three years now.
He's grown up knowing that this was how his life would turn out, and he just gets on with things. He's absolutely brilliant with computers – better than some of the teachers, I think – and he's decided that he wants a career with a computer company. His attitude is so positive that I'm sure he will succeed. He's very artistic, and enjoys drawing. He's also very funny, and he tries not to take his problems too seriously.
As a result, we all like him, and we look after him if he needs help.
I hope that answers your question.
Love
Jo

UNIT OBJECTIVES

TOPICS: technology, science

GRAMMAR: relative clauses

VOCABULARY: computers, science, word building

READING AND USE OF ENGLISH PART 3: word formation

PART 7: multiple matching

WRITING PART 1: using a range of vocabulary

LISTENING PART 1: multiple-choice questions + short recordings

SPEAKING PART 3: structuring a conversation

PART 4: discussing technology

Reading and Use of English

STARTER

Introduce the topic of the first part of the unit by asking students to name all the electronic devices they have in their homes. Note any new vocabulary on the board and offer support with spelling and pronunciation.

1 Focus attention on the photos and elicit answers to the question.

> **Answers**
> A dial-up telephone
> B early mobile phone
> C smartphone
> D smartwatch

2 Before looking at the words in the box, ask students if they can describe any differences in the features of each type of phone. Then put students into pairs to continue the discussion using the words given. Move around the room and offer language support as needed. Compare answers as a class.

> **Suggested answers**
> A dial, landline connection
> B battery, black and white screen, charger, external antenna, heavy weight, mobile network, push buttons, text messaging
> C as B (except black and white screen, external antenna, heavy weight, push buttons) plus: apps, camera, colour screen, GPS, internet, lightweight, touchscreen, wi-fi
> D as C plus: wearable device

3 This task can be done in pairs or as a whole class discussion. Students may need support with extra vocabulary such as *to plug in* (the charger), *to click on* (the icon), *to download* (an antivirus), etc. Encourage students to make a note of any new vocabulary.

4 Encourage students to think about different points of time In the future, such as ten years from now, 30 years from now, etc. and what changes may occur. Remind students to use modal verbs to speculate about what might, could or may happen in the future. Accept all reasonable answers and provide language support as needed.

5 Check understanding of the inventions listed and then put students into small groups to discuss their answers. Tell students to start by saying why and how each one is useful. Encourage them to think about how life would be different for them and their family without each invention. You could use this as an opportunity to practise conditional forms, for example, *If we didn't have a freezer we would have to do the shopping more frequently.* Remind them to give reasons for their ideas and opinions. Then elicit answers from each group and compare ideas across the class.

> **FURTHER PRACTICE**
> Put students into small groups to think of other useful inventions and discuss why they are useful and what they would have to do if they couldn't use them.

Part 7

✅ Exam task

Give students time to read the instructions and then go over the exam tip with the class. Remind them that they should read the texts quickly for general meaning but then read carefully around the parts which they think give the answers to check that the meaning matches the idea in the question.

Allow students 10 to 15 minutes to complete the task under exam conditions before class feedback.

> **Exam task answers**
> 1 B   2 A   3 D   4 B   5 A   6 B   7 C   8 D   9 A   10 C

> **FURTHER PRACTICE**
> Put students into groups to research other new inventions by young people. They can design a brief presentation to give to the rest of the class describing the inventor, their invention and what motivated them to make it.

Grammar

Relative clauses

STARTER
With books closed initiate a class discussion to elicit examples of defining and non-defining relative clauses, relative pronouns and the rules that students remember about how they are used.

Before or after the lesson refer students to the QR code to access *Grammar on the Move*.

1 Students can read the Grammar reference on page 93 before or after doing the exercise. Answers can be checked by referring back to the reading texts.

Answers
1 which   2 who   3 which   4 who   5 which   6 where
7 who   8 which

2 Put students into pairs to discuss their answers to the questions, before going over the rules with the whole class, possibly eliciting more examples of each type of relative clause.

Answers
1   You can omit the relative pronoun in 3 as it is not the subject of the verb which follows it ('One device' is the subject of 'he's invented'), and also in 5 ('a field' is the object of 'he says'). In sentences 1, 2 and 4 the relative pronoun is the subject of the verb which follows, so you can't omit the relative pronoun.
2   You can put *that* in 1–5 (all defining clauses). You cannot use *that* in non-defining clauses.
3   A non-defining clause has commas around it, a defining clause does not.

3 Read through the instructions with the class, checking understanding, and then ask students to complete the gaps on their own or with a partner. When checking answers, ask students to explain what the relative pronoun they chose refers to in each case.

Answers
1   which / that (the subject)
2   whose (the student)
3   which / that / – (the subject)
4   which / that / – (the one – subject)
5   who (less able students)
6   which (these subjects)
7   which (the students will get frustrated with science)
8   who / that (the teachers)

Writing

Part 1 essay

STARTER
Put students into small groups to discuss video games. Encourage them to talk about whether they play games and what the pros and cons of gaming are. Elicit feedback from the class to compare ideas.

1 Read the exam tip with the class and explain that students should check their work after writing to make sure they haven't repeated the same words and that they have used a variety of vocabulary to express their ideas. This preparation exercise focuses on adverbs which can help make their writing more interesting and convey the message more effectively. Give students plenty of time to read the text and then choose the correct adverb, using a dictionary as needed. Check answers as a class. If time allows, ask students to make sentences with the incorrect adverb in each case to check and clarify the meanings.

Answers
1 primarily   2 really   3 just   4 even   5 normally
6 undoubtedly   7 definitely

2 Students work in pairs to discuss their answers to the questions. Go over the answers with the class.

Answers
1   three
2   You don't get any fresh air when you're indoor playing video games.
3   Yes, the essay covers the two points in the essay question and also includes the writer's own idea.

3 Allow time for students to reread the text and make a list of useful vocabulary. Ask them to compare their list with a partner's before checking as a class. Encourage students to add any other words or expressions about gaming which they know.

✓ Exam task

After giving students time to read the question, go through the checklist with the class. Put students into pairs to discuss their ideas and to make a list of useful vocabulary. They can use a dictionary if necessary. Once students have made some notes, they can do the writing at home. Take the work in for individual feedback.

Refer students to the Writing bank on page 96 for further information if needed.

Model answer
The invention of the aeroplane has undoubtedly brought us many advantages. Flights enable us to travel almost anywhere in the world in a much shorter time than by land or by sea. This means people from every different country can meet and communicate relatively easily. Planes also allow us to eat fresh food from all around the world. We can eat many types of fruits and vegetables all year round, rather than just at the times of year they are harvested in our own countries. However, there are downsides to aeroplanes. The main one is their impact on the natural environment. Because they run on fuel that releases a lot of carbon into the atmosphere, they are major contributors to global warming. Furthermore, tourism can create a lot of problems for animal and plant species in regions that attract particularly large numbers of visitors. In spite of such downsides, I would say that aeroplanes have, on balance, been a good thing for human life. However, the invention of the internet, which has completely transformed so much of human life, is even greater than the aeroplane.

Vocabulary – Science

STARTER
With books closed ask students if they can name any different fields of science. Note any new vocabulary on the board.

1 Students work in pairs to do the matching task.

> **Answers**
> 1 ecology   2 electronics   3 psychology   4 chemistry
> 5 astronomy   6 engineering   7 telecommunications
> 8 medicine

2 Give students a few minutes to complete the task before checking answers as a class. Offer support with any new language as needed. Elicit any other words students can add to each list.

> **Answers**
>
> | Topics | Scientific subject |
> | --- | --- |
> | endangered species, conservation, pollution, eco systems | ecology |
> | AI, robotics, computer chips | electronics |
> | acids, gases, metals, atoms, chemical substances | chemistry |
> | cells, human biology, diseases, genetics | medicine |

3 Tell students to think about whether the missing word is singular or plural as they complete the exercise. Check answers as a class.

> **Answers**
> 1 metal   2 gas   3 atom   4 species   5 genetics
> 6 ecosystems

Vocabulary – Word building (3)

4 Elicit or remind students of the task in Reading and Use of English Part 3 and point out that these next exercises will help them prepare for it. Go over the examples with the class, eliciting or modelling the pronunciation of each word and pointing out the stress patterns as well as the spelling changes. Students complete the table on their own or in pairs and then read their answers out to a partner to check pronunciation. Go over the answers with the class, drilling pronunciation as needed.

> **Answers**
>
> | Nouns ending -logy (subjects of study) | biology psychology ecology technology geology |
> | --- | --- |
> | Nouns referring to a person (y + ist) | biologist psychologist ecologist technologist geologist |
> | Adjective (y + ical) | biological psychological ecological technological geological |
> | Adverb (y + ically) | biologically psychologically ecologically technologically geologically |

5 If necessary, go over one or two suffixes with the class, eliciting examples (e.g. *terrible*). Encourage students to think of example words in each category as they work through the exercise individually or with a partner. Check answers as a class, eliciting examples if possible.

> **Answers**
> To make nouns, add: -er, -ity, -ment, -ness, -ship, -sion, -tion
> To make adjectives, add: -al, -ful, -ible, -ic, -ive

6 Point out that students need to establish which type of word is missing from each gap in the exam task before they can change the word given into the appropriate form. This task gives them practice in that. Remind students to read the whole text quickly to get a general idea of the meaning, before reading carefully before and after each gap to make their choice. Students work on their own or in pairs before class feedback.

> **Answers**
> Nouns: 1, 4, 5, 6, 8
> Adjectives: 2, 3, 7

7 Read the second exam tip and, if necessary, remind students that adjectives do not have singular and plural forms. This exercise could be done in stages by first asking students to write the adjective and noun forms for each of the words listed, before choosing which one fits each gap. For example, *relation, relationship, relatable*, etc. Check answers as a class.

> **Answers**
> 1 relationship   2 environmental   3 central   4 probability
> 5 investigations   6 evaluation   7 accessible   8 planners

8 Give students time to read the statement on their own and think about the answer before checking everyone has the right answer.

9 If necessary, go over the first word as an example to check understanding. Then ask students to complete the exercise on their own before checking answers with a partner. When checking answers focus on pronunciation.

Answers

dis-	approval
	honesty
	satisfied
im-	patiently
	polite
il-	legally
in-	experienced
mis-	understanding
un-	believable
	fortunately
	reliable
ir-	regular
	responsible

Part 3

✅ Exam task

Point out to students that they should use the approach they have just practised to do the exam task, i.e. think about what type of word is missing, think about prefixes and suffixes and singular/plural forms. Read through the other two exam tips with the class before allowing them around ten minutes to complete the task under exam conditions, i.e. on their own without conferring. Check answers as a class.

Exam task answers
1 statement   2 unusually   3 evolution   4 relatively
5 combination   6 discoveries   7 ecological   8 sandy

Speaking

Part 3

1 Give students a few minutes to ask and answer the questions, encouraging them to explain their answers. Elicit one or two answers from around the class.

2 🔊 **21** Elicit anything students remember about Speaking Part 3 and point out that this is a typical Part 3 task. Read through the questions before playing the recording. When checking answers, point out that in the exam they may not have time to talk about all the ideas listed as they only have two minutes.

Answers
1 Yes   2 Yes   3 No   4 Yes

Audio script Track 21

Examiner: Now, I'd like you to talk about something together for two minutes. Inventions play an important part in our daily lives. Here are some inventions and a question for you to discuss. First you have some time to look at the task.

Now, talk to each other about how important these inventions are in our daily lives.

Karolina: Shall I begin?

Miguel: OK.

Karolina: Well, I use my laptop every day for my homework and for fun too – I watch films on it and listen to music.

Miguel: Yes, it's the same for me. But computers are also crucial for most people at work and for everything really. Nothing would work without computers.

Karolina: What about the fridge?

Miguel: Food wouldn't last so long without a fridge. But we could live without it, I suppose – it's not so essential.

Karolina: And people would have to go shopping every day so they might waste less food. But they are vital in very hot countries, of course.

Miguel: Yeah, you're right. And we couldn't live without cars, could we? I can't wait to learn to drive. It's so annoying having to get the bus everywhere.

Karolina: Don't you think we ought to try to be less dependent on cars though?

Miguel: That's not going to happen, is it? Lots of people like cycling but I don't think bicycles are a basic necessity in the same way as a car.

Karolina: I agree, although I think in some countries, they are more important as a way of travelling. Most people live in cities though, and cycling can be dangerous in traffic.

Miguel: The last thing to talk about is a TV. What do you think about that?

Karolina: Well, it's not so significant now because you can watch TV on your computer or even your phone.

Miguel: But you can't sit down and watch a film with friends on a phone. It's too small!

Karolina: That's true.

Miguel: I would miss my TV. I like lying on the sofa in front of it when I'm tired.

3 🔊 **21** Read through the functions listed and tell students to listen to the recording again and make a note of the exact words the candidates use for each function. They may be able to hear more than one example phrase for each one. Check answers as a class and elicit any other expressions students can think of for each function. For example, *Would you like to start*?

Answers
1 'Shall I begin?'
2 'What about the … ?' 'The last thing to talk about is a …'
3 'Don't you think … ?' 'What do you think about that?'
4 '… it's the same for me', '… you're right', 'I agree, although I think …', 'That's true.'

4 Refer students back to the task, if necessary, to remind them that the question asked how important the inventions are. Point out that they should try to use a range of language when speaking, just like in writing. Give students time to brainstorm as many synonyms of *important* as they can. Go over answers with the class and encourage students to make a note of any words they did not think of.

> **Suggested answers**
> serious, urgent, significant, crucial, vital, essential, a necessity

5 🔊 **21** Play the recording again for students to make a note of the words the candidates use. Check answers as a class.

> **Answers**
> '… computers are also crucial for most people at work …'
> '(A fridge is) not so essential.'
> '(Fridges) are vital in very hot countries …'
> '… I don't think bicycles are a basic necessity …'
> '(TV's) not so significant now …'

6 🔊 **22** Ask students what happens in the exam after the two-minute discussion. If necessary, remind them they have one minute to answer another question with their partner. Read the two questions and play the recording before class feedback.

> **Answers**
> Karolina thinks the TV and the laptop, and Miguel thinks the bicycle and the laptop. They don't agree on both things and it doesn't matter.

Audio script Track 22	
Examiner:	Now you have a minute to decide which two inventions will become less important in the future.
Karolina:	Do you want to start?
Miguel:	Well, I think we've already said that the bicycle isn't as important in people's lives as the others, so I think that will definitely become less important.
Karolina:	It might not if we have special cycle lanes in towns. And hopefully people will get greener, so they might all buy bicycles – even you!
Miguel:	I suppose so. Which would you choose then?
Karolina:	I think people will stop watching TV in their living rooms, so the traditional TV might disappear. I choose the TV and maybe the laptop because that's the same really – people can do everything on their phone or a tablet and they won't need a TV, a laptop and a phone as well.
Miguel:	Well, I still think the bicycle will be less important but I agree with you about the laptop. I think they're probably too big and heavy to carry about. So, we don't quite agree.
Examiner:	Thank you.

7 🔊 **22** Tell students to make notes of the actual words the candidates use as they listen to the recording again. Check answers as a class.

> **Answers**
> 1 She asks Miguel: 'Do you want to start?'
> 2 'Which would you choose then?'
> 3 'I still think …'

✓ Exam task

Read the exam tip with the class and, if necessary, refer them to the earlier units to revise the useful language before they start. They can also use some of the expressions they heard on the two recordings. Point out that this question also asks how important something is, so they should try to include some of the synonyms they learnt to avoid repeating the word *important*. Finally, remind students not to answer the second question during the initial two-minute discussion. Move around the class monitoring as students speak, and then hold a feedback session to praise and comment on any common errors after they finish.

Refer students to the Speaking bank on page 114 for further information if needed.

Part 4

✓ Exam task

Go over the exam tip reminding students that in Speaking Part 4 they have the opportunity to demonstrate how good their English is without the strict time constraints of the rest of the exam so they should always try to give extended answers. However, it is also important that they stay focused on the question and finish what they want to say in an appropriate and clear way, using falling intonation, for example. In the exam, Part 4 lasts four minutes, but here they can take a few minutes longer so they have the chance to discuss their answers to all the questions. Encourage students to comment on whether they agree or disagree with their partner's ideas.

Refer students to the Speaking bank on page 116 for further information if needed.

Listening

Part 1

> **STARTER**
> Elicit anything students remember about Listening Part 1. Ask a few questions if necessary. For example, *How many recordings do you hear?* (eight), *Are the recordings connected to each other?* (no), *How many speakers do you hear in each recording?* (one or two), *How many times do you hear each recording?* (twice).

1 Draw attention to the exam task and the exam tip before giving students time to do this exercise. Students check their answers with a partner before class feedback.

> **Answers**
> A4   B5   C3   D1   E8   F6   G2   H7

🔊 ㉓ As students have already had the chance to read through the questions, play the recording straight away and ask them to complete the task under exam conditions. Go through the answers with the class.

Exam task answers
1 C 2 B 3 A 4 C 5 A 6 A 7 B 8 B

FURTHER PRACTICE

If time allows, photocopy the audio script and ask students to underline the sections which give the correct answer in one colour and the reasons why the other two answers are wrong in another colour. This can help them understand the mechanism of this type of listening task and the way that words and phrases can be used to distract them from the correct answers.

Audio script Track 23

You will hear people talking in eight different situations. For questions 1–8, choose the best answer, A, B or C.

1

You hear a boy who lived in Spain telling a friend in England about his New Year's Eve.

Boy: To be honest, I didn't use to look forward to New Year's Eve in Spain, when the clock strikes midnight, because then, you're supposed to eat 12 grapes – one for each strike of the clock. My mum would take the skin off the grapes for me, but there's just no way a kid can eat 12 grapes in a few seconds. Now I'm older and it's easier for me, I appreciate the tradition a bit more because it's so hilarious to see adults looking silly with their mouths full of grapes – no one can stay serious when they see that – so it's good from that point of view.

2

You hear a boy telling his friend about going on a ghost walk in London.

Girl: What did you do on your trip to London?

Boy: Ooh, lots. Including one of those ghost walks around the city!

Girl: What, so you went to places where people are supposed to have seen ghosts?

Boy: Yeah.

Girl: I don't think I could do that; I'd be too scared.

Boy: Well, it wasn't my idea, it was my sister's. I didn't fancy wandering around old places for two hours, so tried to persuade her to do something else, but she wouldn't.

Girl: So how was it?

Boy: Well, we didn't see any ghosts, which of course came as no surprise.

3

You hear a girl talking to her father about music lessons.

Dad: Your mum says you want to learn the cello, bass guitar and trumpet, Celia – but we can't afford lessons for three instruments. You're going to have to choose one.

Celia: Well, that's OK, Dad. I'm teaching myself the bass guitar anyway, and can play along with loads of songs now.

Dad: I know, but wouldn't you like to learn some more advanced techniques?

Celia: Not as much as I want to give the cello a try. And I've gone off the idea of the trumpet – two of my friends have taken it up and I'd rather not do the same as them.

Dad: Right. Let's arrange some lessons with the teacher then.

4

You hear two friends talking about a school football match.

Girl: You saw our team win the final of the schools' championship yesterday, didn't you?

Boy: Yeah, they were incredible. Your sister scored one of the goals, didn't she?

Girl: The third one, yeah. I was so proud!

Boy: I bet, and the goalie was brilliant, too – didn't let in any goals.

Girl: Despite the other team attacking all the time – they got close to scoring a few times, but she stayed so cool.

Boy: Yeah, the result could have been very different without her.

Girl: I don't know, the rest of the team were really strong too.

5

You hear a boy talking about the geography course he's doing.

Boy: The thing about this course is that it's the only one I know that has so many field trips – you know, visits to places to study specific things. Like, we went to the Black Mountains to gather data on the micro-climate there, and to the coast to study the rock in the cliffs – and that was just in the first term. I considered loads of other geography courses before choosing this one, and there was no contest really – the rest had too much classroom time, and not nearly enough practical research outdoors.

6

You hear the introduction to a podcast about waste plastic.

There's a widespread awareness of the problem that plastic waste causes globally, and you hear a lot of stories in the media about how terrible the situation is. This podcast doesn't tell that sort of story; it's focus is how people all around the world are developing innovative ways of removing plastic waste from their environment and putting it to good use. For instance, waste plastic is the perfect building material in many ways: there's plenty of it, it's easily shaped, it lasts a long time and its waterproof. That's why it's being used to construct schools, homes and community buildings in countries from Canada to the Ivory Coast.

7

You hear a boy talking to his mother about a jacket he's just got.

Mum: I don't think I've seen that jacket before, have I?

Boy: No, it's new. Well, not brand new – second hand.

Mum: Oh yes, from the charity shop. I'd forgotten that's where you and your friends were planning to go this morning.

Boy: Actually, there was one like this in the shop, but then my mate Pedro said he had one exactly the same that didn't fit him – he'd ordered it online and it was too small when it arrived. No idea why he didn't send it back.

Mum: That's the problem with getting stuff online. Anyway, lucky for you!

Boy: Yeah! I picked it up on my way home.

8

You hear a report on a science event.

The aim of Science Now is to give secondary-school students the chance to develop their passion for science and to encourage collaboration, communication and creativity.

We're pleased to report that 12 teams, each supported by a teacher, took part this year, and the topic was physics. Their task was to create a piece of art that could teach an aspect of science to people their age. We had a wide range of entries, from videos to sculptures made of rubbish. Judging was extremely difficult, but in the end the trophy was awarded to Greendale Academy for their superb model of a star being created in space.

Revision answer key

UNIT 1

1 1 I don't understand   2 're camping   3 recognise
4 be sitting   5 I arrive   6 'm cleaning   7 you hear
8 come

2 1 are not / aren't as/so wide as
2 far more noise
3 is much longer than / takes much more time than
4 like best is not / isn't far
5 less often than

3 1 C   2 B   3 C   4 A   5 B   6 D   7 A   8 D

4 1 will be   2 arrive   3 arrives   4 think   5 take
6 I've done   7 come   8 I am   9 know   10 'm staying
11 like   12 will be   13 I've   14 Is there   15 live

UNIT 2

1 1 d was running
2 f had already closed
3 h had
4 b haven't / have not managed
5 a didn't / did not answer
6 g haven't / have not bought
7 c sent
8 e hasn't / has not been

2 1 goes
2 're/are
3 'll/will be / 'm/am going to be
4 'll/will let
5 invited
6 'd/had never skateboarded
7 set
8 was shining
9 've/have been having / had
10 knew

3 1 excitedly   2 definitely   3 easily   4 immediately
5 usually   6 carefully   7 simply   8 particularly

4 1 mysterious   2 natural   3 adventurous   4 reliable
5 suitable   6 furious   7 predictable   8 central

UNIT 3

1 1 While / Although   2 Even though   3 Although
4 Although   5 In spite of   6 Even though   7 Despite
8 Although

2 1 was cancelled
2 'm/am being sent
3 was told / 've/have been told
4 has been organised / is being organised / was organised
5 will be delivered
6 is being made
7 is being displayed / is going to be displayed
8 were returned

3 1 sound technician   2 scriptwriter   3 live performance
4 producer   5 camera operator   6 director
7 costume designer   8 set designer

4 1 science fiction   2 comedy   3 thriller   4 documentary
5 western   6 cartoon   7 animation   8 horror
9 action   10 romantic comedy

5 1 possible answers: (bass) guitar, cello, violin, harp
2 (music) critics
3 possible answers: pop, heavy metal, classical, punk,
salsa, hip-hop, rock and roll, jazz, rap, soul
4 manager
5 lyrics
6 track
7 beat
8 fans

UNIT 4

1 1 B   2 A   3 B   4 C   5 B   6 A   7 B   8 C

2 1 of   2 about   3 to   4 in   5 on   6 for   7 with
8 about   9 about   10 of/in

3 1 pitch   2 referee   3 goalkeeper's   4 defenders
5 tackle

4 1 convenience   2 equality   3 generous
4 independence   5 patient   6 conclusion
7 connection   8 divide   9 expansion   10 persuade

UNIT 5

1 1 i had been   2 g 'd/would have missed out   3 e is
   4 d starts   5 j would be   6 h prepares   7 c go
   8 b buy   9 a start/started   10 f don't get

2 1 secondary   2 majority   3 exam/examination
   4 comprehensive   5 ability   6 challenging   7 variety
   8 possibility   9 choice   10 application(s)

3 1 out   2 out   3 on   4 up   5 in   6 up

UNIT 6

1 1 a   2 –   3 –   4 the   5 the   6 –   7 the   8 –   9 The
   10 a   11 the   12 –/the   13 –   14 the   15 –/the
   16 the   17 a   18 –   19 the   20 an

2 1 such a beautiful
   2 so excited
   3 so beautiful
   4 so good
   5 such a marvellous day
   6 such a tasty stew
   7 such good memories
   8 such a good time
   9 so important
   10 such a great goal

3 1 air conditioning
   2 electrical equipment
   3 email attachment
   4 fresh ingredients/produce
   5 local produce/ingredients
   6 plastic bags
   7 ready meals
   8 recycled paper
   9 reduce waste
   10 take a shower

4 1 reduce waste
   2 take a shower
   3 electrical equipment
   4 recycled paper
   5 email attachment
   6 air conditioning
   7 plastic bags
   8 local produce
   9 fresh ingredients
   10 ready meals

UNIT 7

1 1 green product   2 Vintage clothing   3 sale item
   4 Imported goods   5 consumer   6 brand

2 1 amused   2 irritated   3 furious   4 astonished
   5 concerned   6 anxious

3 1 to go   2 to fall   3 to do   4 taking   5 swimming
   6 relaxing   7 driving   8 to find   9 putting   10 go
   11 looking   12 to go

4 1 explained (that) he couldn't
   2 agreed to help / agreed (that) she would help
   3 so I can't come
   4 hadn't / had not seen such a
   5 told me (that) she liked
   6 if I knew

UNIT 8

1 1 who   2 whose   3 which/that   4 who/that   5 where
   6 where   7 which   8 which/that/–

2 1 e   2 c   3 f   4 a   5 b   6 d

3 1 strength   2 attractive   3 originally   4 possibilities
   5 misunderstanding   6 powerful   7 commercials
   8 impolite

Grammar reference answer key

UNIT 1

1 1 are taking up 2 helps 3 use up 4 walk 5 go
6 'm training 7 spend / 'm spending

2 1 go 2 'm/am meeting 3 don't reply 4 's/is becoming
5 's/is helping 6 Do; prefer

3 1 Her musical talent has always been greater than her
sister's.

2 His results throughout the competition were as
impressive as the scores of his nearest rival.

3 The lecturer is less available to his students since he
started attending conferences every month.

4 The plants are not growing as fast as my friends
predicted.

5 Her interest in history is considerably greater now than
it was at the beginning of her degree.

6 Their daughter doesn't live quite as close to them as
they would ideally want.

7 There are slightly more people living in the village than
five years ago.

8 It's considerably more environmentally friendly to travel
by train than by plane.

UNIT 2

1 1 Correct

2 Incorrect. The teacher quickly explained the task to the
students.

3 Correct

4 Correct

5 Incorrect. Susan happily sang her favourite song as she
got ready to go out.

6 Correct

2 1 was listening 2 often phoned 3 realised
4 was shining; were singing 5 won

3 1 was packing; found

2 was leaving; realised

3 was practising; watched / was watching

4 heard; stopped; were doing; looked

5 crashed; was writing

4 1 had/'d been waiting 2 had/'d been writing
3 had/'d baked 4 had/'d handed 5 had/'d already read
6 had/'d picked up

5 1 had not / hadn't ordered 2 had/'d tried
3 had/'d fallen 4 had/'d been playing tennis
5 had/'d been reading 6 had/'d lived

6 1 didn't use to enjoy 2 didn't use to do 3 used to spend
4 used to own 5 Did (she) use to keep 6 didn't use to
like

7 1 used to play / played 2 used to work / worked
3 used to enjoy / enjoyed 4 used to live / lived
5 Correct 6 Correct

UNIT 3

1 1 Incorrect. Michael didn't get a sports scholarship even
though he's really good at basketball.

2 Incorrect. Despite having an injury last year, / Despite his
injury last year, Scott was able to compete in the world
championships.

3 Incorrect. In spite of leaving the house really early, / In
spite of the fact that we left the house really early, we
still missed our flight.

4 Correct

5 Correct

2 1 A 2 C 3 C 4 B 5 C 6 A

UNIT 4

1 1 Could 2 couldn't 3 can 4 was able to 5 can't
6 can't

2 1 ~~wasn't able translate~~ wasn't able to translate
2 ~~fortunately I could~~ fortunately I was able to
3 ~~I couldn't accept it~~ I can't accept it
4 Correct
5 Correct
6 ~~She could run~~ She was able to / managed to run

3 1 ~~shouldn't have ate~~ shouldn't have eaten
2 ~~should arrived~~ should have arrived
3 ~~should have listen~~ should have listened
4 ~~People ought waste~~ People ought to waste
5 ~~should to ask~~ should ask

4 1 could 2 can't have 3 have to 4 must 5 must
6 couldn't 7 didn't need to 8 can

5 1 on 2 on 3 on 4 at 5 in; on 6 at

UNIT 5

1 1 is; 'll/will have to   2 were; 'd/would buy   3 come; will see   4 had; wouldn't be   5 improves; 'll/will have to   6 'd/would go; won

2 1 C   2 C   3 C   4 A   5 B   6 B

3 1 hadn't / had not arrived; wouldn't / would not have missed

2 'd/had come; wouldn't / would not have got up

3 'd/had worked; might have got

4 'd/had been; would've / would have learnt

5 hadn't / had not boarded; 'd/would never have met

6 would've / would have caught; 'd/had had

4 1 had   2 could meet   3 would stop   4 would start   5 had   6 wouldn't / would not keep

5 1 was   2 would stop   3 knew   4 could play   5 knew   6 wouldn't roll

UNIT 6

1 1 ~~some suitable accommodations~~ some suitable accommodation

2 ~~our luggages~~ our luggage

3 ~~A pollution~~ Pollution

4 ~~an advice~~ advice / any advice

5 Correct

6 ~~work of art~~ works of art

2 1 coffee   2 accommodation   3 cardboard; paper   4 was   5 equipment; is   6 damage

3 1 a; the   2 the; the; a; the   3 an; the   4 the   5 the   6 a; the

4 1 so   2 such a   3 so   4 so   5 such a

5 1 ~~enough hot~~ hot enough

2 ~~too late catch~~ too late to catch

3 ~~medicine enough~~ enough medicine

4 ~~enough fit~~ fit enough

5 ~~enough dark~~ too dark

UNIT 7

1 1 ~~He decided buy~~ He decided to buy

2 Correct

3 ~~They promised visiting~~ They promised to visit

4 Correct

5 ~~She expected not getting the job~~ She expected not to get the job / She didn't expect to get the job

6 ~~luckily managed finish~~ luckily managed to finish

2 1 to chat   2 to doing   3 being   4 lying   5 accepting   6 talking   7 to go

3 1 A   2 A   3 B   4 B   5 A   6 A

UNIT 8

1 1 which   2 whose   3 which   4 where   5 who   6 who

2 1 that/which   2 where   3 that/which   4 that/who   5 that/who   6 whose

3 1 The music that/which Sandra was playing last night was by Beethoven.

2 The flute that/which Sandra was playing in the concert was not hers.

3 Luke, whose flute Sandra borrowed, is her music teacher.

4 We've just listened to Sandra's latest recording, which is in the top ten in the classical charts.

5 Sandra's mother, who was in the audience tonight, is very proud of her.

6 Tomorrow, Sandra is going back to London, where she goes to music school.

4 1 She spent a semester in Toulouse so that she could improve her French.

2 He is taking part in a training course in order that he can improve his project management skills.

3 I left the office early in order to avoid the rush-hour traffic.

4 Martha washed all of her dirty dishes so as not to annoy her housemates.

5 You should wear warm clothes in order not to catch a cold in the winter.

Writing bank answer key

Part 1: essay

1

Question: Will environmental problems be worse in 20 years?
Ideas: pollution, climate change and your own idea

2

It includes the extra idea of a growing population.

3

Ideas 1, 3, 4, 6, 8

4 1 sentence 1   2 sentences 3, 6   3 sentences 4, 8

5 1 B. It makes general statements to introduce the topic and the arguments which will be developed in the essay.
   2 C. It sums up arguments on both sides.

7 1 as   2 in my opinion   3 In addition to this
   4 Firstly   5 such as

9

Model answer
Cycling is becoming a very popular way of getting around cities nowadays, and a lot of big cities have cycle schemes which allow people to use public bikes. But there are advantages and disadvantages to bikes as a form of city transport.
On the one hand, cycling is good for your health. It provides good exercise, and can help you to lose weight and keep fit. It is also cheap, because if you have your own bike, it does not cost you anything to travel around the city. A third advantage is that cycling is good for the environment, because it does not cause any pollution.
On the other hand, cycling on busy streets can be dangerous. Car and lorry drivers do not always notice cyclists, especially when it is dark, and this can lead to accidents.
On balance, I would say that cycling is an excellent form of transport in cities during the day and when the weather is nice. However, when it is dark or the weather is bad, I think that buses and trains are a better option.

Part 2: email / letter

1

You should write an email to a friend, Jo. You should write about your new home, things there are to do in the city and your new friends.

2

Yes, it answers all the questions in Jo's email. The tone is informal.

3 1 false   2 true   3 true   4 false   5 true   6 false

4

Sentences 2, 5, 6 and 8. They are suitable because they are formal.

5 1 Dear Ms Copeland
   2 in response to
   3 currently
   4 would be interested in working
   5 studied different aspects of
   6 was employed
   7 gained some experience as
   8 customer satisfaction
   9 I would be grateful if you would
   10 I look forward to hearing from you.

7 1 It was great **to** hear from you.
   2 Why **don't you** come
   3 I would **be** able to help
   4 I look forward **to** hearing from you.

9

Model answer
Dear Ms Simpson,
I am writing in response to your job advertisement, which appeared in the *Weekly News* last week.
I am interested in applying for the job of receptionist at your hotel this summer. This role interests me particularly because I am a very friendly and outgoing person, and I would enjoy meeting guests and helping them feel welcome. As I am currently studying English, it would also be a good opportunity for me to practise using the language.
I have experience of working as a hotel receptionist, as I spent last summer working in a hotel in Ireland. I am therefore used to taking reservations, helping guests check in and check out and dealing with problems they may have. I am cheerful and hardworking, and I understand the importance of providing good customer service. I am also a good team worker, which I know is a very important quality for working in a busy hotel. I have a good level of English, and I am able to communicate well in the language.
I hope you will consider me for this role, and I look forward to hearing from you.
Lisa Bianchi

Part 2: review

You should write a review of a film you have seen. You should say what it is about, say why you did or didn't enjoy it, and say whether you think other people will enjoy it. People will read your review in an English-language magazine.

2 1 yes   2 yes   3 anyone who enjoys fantasy movies
4 informal and friendly

3

Plan A is better. Each paragraph has a clear topic and gives the reader useful and helpful information; it starts with a general introduction with factual information; it gives good points and problems about the website/product; it ends with a clear recommendation. Plan B contains information that is not relevant for the reader, e.g. the writer needed a new tablet, how the writer found the website; the third heading is not appropriate, as the focus should be the product you bought, not games that you play; it doesn't end with a clear recommendation.

4 1 c   2 f   3 a   4 e   5 d   6 b

5 1 spite   2 though   3 despite   4 Although   5 However

7 1 than   2 disappointing   3 will   4 miss   5 using
6 advise

9
Model answer
Playa de Oro
Last summer, I spent a week with my family in a holiday resort called Playa de Oro in the south of Spain. This is a popular tourist area, but we were keen to choose a quiet resort where we could just relax on the beach or by the pool.
The resort had some positive points. The apartment buildings were attractive, and our apartment was spacious and well-equipped. The resort had two swimming pools, and both were extremely clean and well-maintained. The staff were also incredibly friendly and helpful.
However, we were disappointed to find that our resort was surrounded by several other, much bigger resorts. The beach was therefore absolutely packed with people every day, and it was almost impossible to find a place to sit. Even worse, the advert said that the resort was peaceful, but in fact there were two nightclubs nearby which were open every night until four o'clock in the morning! We hardly slept, and came home exhausted.
This resort might be OK if you want a week-long party, but my advice is to avoid it if you want a peaceful, relaxing holiday.

Part 2: article

You should write an article about your hobby. You should say what it is, how you started doing it, and why you enjoy it. People will read your article in an English-language magazine.

2 1 yes   2 four   3 one   4 informal

B is the best. The title is interesting and makes the reader think. The first sentence is a question which engages the reader and makes them think for themselves about Mandela's achievements.

4 1 d   2 e   3 a

5 1 fascinated by   2 packed   3 huge   4 freezing
5 terrifying   6 absolutely essential

6 2 I like is   3 that/which really surprised me was
4 I will never forget is   5 I noticed was

8 1 For   2 in   3 as   4 which   5 tell   6 What

10
Model answer
A healthy life is a happy life
Can you be happy if you're not fit and healthy? For me, the answer to this question is definitely no, and keeping fit and healthy is an important part of life.
Firstly, a good diet is vital if you want to maintain a healthy life. This means eating plenty of fruit and vegetables, and avoiding foods high in fat and sugar. It can be difficult to achieve this if you eat out in restaurants, where portions tend to be large and the food is often rich. However, it is possible to maintain a balanced diet if you make careful choices.
The second important part of a healthy lifestyle is exercise. There are obviously hundreds of different ways to exercise, from running and hiking to playing football and tennis, but in my opinion, the most important thing is to find a form of exercise that you enjoy. After all, no one can motivate themselves to do something every week if it isn't fun!
By eating sensibly and doing regular exercise, it is possible for anyone to improve their health, and remember – healthier people are happier people!

Part 2: report

The report is for the group leader of some English-speaking students. The report should include: the best time of year to visit your city, interesting places to visit, and the best way to travel around the city.

2

Yes, it covers all the points in the exam task.

3 1 c 2 a 3 b

4
B. The information is relevant to the topic of the report and uses personal experience to support the recommendation.

5
Introduction: C. It explains the aim accurately and uses formal language. (A is too informal; B is not accurate, as the report does not discuss disadvantages.)
Conclusion: A. It gives a clear recommendation and uses formal language. (B is too informal; C does not give a clear recommendation.)

6 1 is often recommended 2 is considered to be
3 is expected 4 has been suggested 5 are recommended

8 1 The aim **of** this report 2 In **addition** to this
3 college. **M**oreover, the ones 4 I have no hesitation in
recommending 5 All things **considered**, the
6 In conclusion,

10
Model answer
Introduction
The aim of this report is to look at the shops in a popular shopping centre in Oxford and make recommendations for improvements.
Green Cross Shopping Centre
Green Cross is a large and popular shopping centre near the city centre. It has nearly 150 shops, as well as several cafés and restaurants.
Popular shops
The most popular shops are the large clothes shops, especially those selling well-known brands of clothing. A lot of these shops offer significant discounts throughout the year, which makes them popular with shoppers who are searching for bargains. The more exclusive stores offer additional services such as fashion advice, which makes them attractive to customers who are looking for something special.
Recommendations for improvements
Some smaller independent shops would be a good addition. There are very few of these at present, and they would offer shoppers a good alternative to the big High Street names.
Conclusion
To sum up, Green Cross is a busy and successful shopping centre, which already has plenty of popular shops. It could be improved by having some smaller stores offering more unusual alternatives to the standard brands.

Part 2: story

2 1 Feeling slightly nervous, Emma walked up the steps and onto the plane. 2 bad weather and a surprise
3 On an English-language website

3 1 yes 2 yes 3 yes 4 past simple, past continuous and past perfect 5 yes

5
Answer B is better. It gives some background information (there was no one else on the train, someone had left the bag), it includes a description which helps the reader have a picture in their mind (a modern, fashionable bag) and it includes some suspense (it doesn't say immediately that it was a phone in the bag that was ringing). It also uses a wider range of verb forms, and a wider range of vocabulary.

6
Answer A is best because it gives a clear ending to the story. Laura had obviously spoken to the woman and they had arranged to meet. There are no more questions to answer. Answer B doesn't give a clear ending. We don't know why the woman suddenly appeared, and we don't know that it is definitely her bag. It doesn't feel like an ending because it feels as if something else is going to happen, e.g. the woman will call the police.

8 1 'Will you come with me?' he asked.
2 'Don't worry,' he said.
3 'Get out!' she cried.
4 'It doesn't matter,' she said.

10
Model answer
The wrong number
When he saw the postman coming up to his door, Matt ran to open it. His phone had broken the week before, and he was expecting a new one. He and his parents had recently moved to a small village, and he was missing his old friends in London. There didn't seem to be any young people here! Matt unpacked the phone, quickly tapped in his friend Oli's number, then waited excitedly.
'Hello,' a voice said, but it wasn't Oli's.
'Who are you?' Matt asked. 'And where's Oli?'
'I don't know anyone called Oli,' the boy replied. 'I live in a little village called Norton, and there's definitely no one called Oli here.'
'You live in Norton?' Matt said, amazed. 'So do I!'
'Hooray!' the boy replied. 'You must be the new boy at number 42. I live at number 37. Look out of your window!'
Matt walked to the window and saw a boy in the house opposite, waving to him.
'How amazing!' said Matt. 'I didn't think there were any young people here! Maybe I'll make some friends after all!'

Speaking bank answer key

Part 1

3 1 a   2 c   3 e   4 a   5 b   6 d   7 d   8 c   9 e   10 b

4

Yes, she does.

🔊 **24**

Examiner:	What do you like about your hometown?
Sofia:	Well, I'm from Milan, in the north of Italy. It's a big city, and I enjoy living there because there's always lots to do, like going to the cinema or music concerts. There are also a lot of young people there, so I like that as well.
Examiner:	What do you enjoy doing in your free time?
Sofia:	Well, I'm quite a sporty person, so I do a lot of exercise. For example, I go to the gym two or three times a week, and I play tennis. I also enjoy spending time with my friends.
Examiner:	Which country would you most like to visit?
Sofia:	I would love to go to Australia. The reason for this is that I like hot weather and I love going to the beach. The beaches in Australia look amazing. I also think the way of life in Australia is quite relaxed – having barbecues and things like that, so I think I'd enjoy that.
Examiner:	Which subject did you most enjoy when you were at school?
Sofia:	Could you repeat that, please?
Examiner:	Yes. Which subject did you most enjoy when you were at school?
Sofia:	That was definitely geography, because I'm really interested in different countries, and I love learning about how people live in other parts of the world. I had a very good geography teacher at school too, and I think he made the subject very interesting.

5 1 past   2 present   3 future   4 present   5 future
6 past

6 1 C   2 A   3 C   4 B   5 C   6 B

7

adding extra information: also, as well, plus, too
giving a reason: because, the reason for this is that
giving an example: for example, for instance, like, such as

8 1 The reason for this is that   2 too   3 because   4 like
5 For instance,   6 also

🔊 **25**

Examiner:	In what ways do you think you will use English in the future?
Dan:	I think I'll use English for my job in the future. The reason for this is that I want to work for an international company, so probably everyone will speak English to each other. I'll probably use it for travelling too, because I'd like to travel and visit lots of different countries.
Examiner:	What do you usually do on your birthday?

Dan:	I usually see my family on my birthday because they like to wish me a happy birthday and they might have presents for me. Then in the evening I usually get together with some friends and do something, like go for a meal together.
Examiner:	What kind of music do you enjoy listening to?
Dan:	I really enjoy R&B music. For instance, I like American singers like Rihanna. I'm also keen on classical music because I find it very relaxing.

Part 2

3

The topic is holidays. You have to say why the people have chosen these holidays.

4

Yes, for both photographs.

🔊 **26**

Examiner:	In this part of the test I'm going to give each of you two photographs. I'd like you to talk about your photographs on your own for about a minute, and also to answer a question about your partner's photographs. Tanya, it's your turn first. Here are your photographs. They show people on holiday. I'd like you to compare the photographs and say why you think the people chose these holidays.
Tanya:	Both pictures show people on holiday, but they're different kinds of holidays. The people in the first photo are in the countryside, whereas the second photo shows a big city. It looks as if the people in the first photo are on a walking holiday, because they've got backpacks and a map. On the other hand, the other people are probably doing some sightseeing. They seem to be up in a tower, and they're taking a selfie. Another difference is that the people in the city look happy and relaxed, whereas the people in the countryside look worried. I think they might be lost. They don't look as happy as the people on the city break. I think the people in the first photo must enjoy walking. Maybe they chose this holiday because they enjoy being in the countryside. I think the people in the second photo enjoy city life, so I guess they probably chose to visit this city because there are lots of interesting things to see.

5 1 Both   2 different   3 whereas   4 other   5 difference
6 as

🔊 **27**

Narrator:	1
Tanya:	Both pictures show people on holiday.
Narrator:	2
Tanya:	They're different kinds of holidays.
Narrator:	3
Tanya:	The people in the first photo are in the countryside, whereas the second photo shows a big city.
Narrator:	4
Tanya:	On the other hand, the other people are probably doing some sightseeing.

Narrator:	5
Tanya:	Another difference is that the people in the city look happy and relaxed.
Narrator:	6
Tanya:	They don't look as happy as the people on the city break.

6 1c 2e 3a 4f 5b 6d 7h 8g

🔊 **28**

Narrator:	1
Tanya:	It looks as if they're on a walking holiday.
Narrator:	2
Tanya:	They're probably doing some sightseeing.
Narrator:	3
Tanya:	They seem to be up in a tower.
Narrator:	4
Tanya:	They look happy and relaxed.
Narrator:	5
Tanya:	I think they might be lost.
Narrator:	6
Tanya:	They must enjoy walking.
Narrator:	7
Tanya:	Maybe they chose this holiday because they enjoy being in the countryside.
Narrator:	8
Tanya:	I guess they probably chose to visit this city because there are lots of interesting things to see.

7 Speaker 1 – B   Speaker 2 – D   Speaker 3 – A

🔊 **29**

Narrator:	Speaker 1
Student 1:	These two photos both show people cooking food. I prefer the first photo because it shows a dad cooking with his children. I think they might be making a cake or something. He looks very happy, and the children are both looking very serious, so I guess they're concentrating on what they're doing. I think that when they eat the cake, they will all feel very proud that they made it together. I think it's really nice for parents to spend time in this way with their children. The second photo shows a chef in a restaurant.
Narrator:	Speaker 2
Student 2:	Both photos show people preparing food. The first photo shows a dad cooking with his children, whereas the second photo shows a professional chef cooking in a restaurant. The main difference between the two photos is that the dad is cooking for pleasure, whereas the chef is cooking because it's his job. The dad probably only cooks from time to time. On the other hand, the chef probably cooks every day. The people in both photos look quite happy, although the children look a bit serious. The chef looks as if he enjoys his work, but I think it's much more fun when you're cooking just for pleasure, rather than cooking as a job. I think the professional chef must get very hot sometimes, and he might get a bit fed up with his job sometimes, because chefs often have to work late at night. I would prefer to just cook at home, for fun, or to cook meals for my friends.
Narrator:	3
Student 3:	The first photo shows a dad with his children. I think they're at home, and they're making a cake together. The dad is smiling and he's looking very relaxed and happy.

The two children look a bit serious, but I'm sure they're looking forward to eating the cake. Personally, I love making cakes at home. The second photo shows a chef in a restaurant. He's cooking a big pan of something, but I can't see what it is. He looks like he is concentrating on what he is doing, so I think he is taking a lot of care with the food he's preparing. I wouldn't like to be a professional chef because I think it's very hard work!

8

🔊 **30**

Student:	Both photos show people working, but their jobs are very different. The first photo shows two factory workers, making a car, whereas the second photo shows a doctor treating a child. The factory workers might be quite bored. I guess this kind of work is quite boring because you probably do the same thing all day, whereas a doctor's job changes all the time. I think the doctor's job is quite sociable, whereas the people in the first photo are working with a piece of machinery rather than with people. I think that in both jobs the people have a lot of responsibility. I think the factory job must be difficult because you have to concentrate a lot, to make sure you do it properly, but it isn't very interesting. I think the doctor's job is more difficult because sometimes you see people who are very ill, which might be upsetting.

Part 3

3

You have to discuss how the different ideas might attract more guests to a hotel. There are five prompts to discuss.

4

They discuss all the prompts. Yes, they both express their opinions.

🔊 **31**

Examiner:	Now, I'd like you to talk about something together for about two minutes. I'd like you to imagine that a hotel wants to attract more guests. Here are some ideas they're thinking about. Talk to each other about why these ideas would attract more guests to the hotel.
Paul:	Shall we start with tennis courts? This sounds like a good idea. A lot of people like playing tennis.
Eva:	I can see what you mean, but not everyone likes tennis, and a lot of people go on holiday to relax, so they perhaps don't want to do sport. I think a swimming pool might be a better idea, because people of all ages can use a swimming pool. Do you agree?
Paul:	Yes, you're right. I hadn't thought about that. I agree that a swimming pool's a good idea because people like to sit by it even if they don't swim. … What do you think about the idea of reduced prices? I think that would make a difference.
Eva:	Yes, that's true. There are so many hotels to choose from, and people usually look at the price and try to find a bargain. But I'm not sure that price is enough on its own because people are often happy to pay a bit more money for a hotel with better facilities.
Paul:	Yes, I agree. I think evening entertainment might be a good idea, though. That's a bit different, too, because not many hotels offer it.

Eva:	Yes, and it would be good if they offered entertainment for children too, not just adults.
Paul:	Yes, I completely agree with you. Do you think that having an award-winning chef would attract customers?
Eva:	Yes, I do. Everyone loves good food, but a lot of hotels don't have very good restaurants. They could also open the restaurant to everyone, but offer cheaper prices for guests.
Paul:	That's a good idea. I think that would definitely encourage more people to stay at the hotel.

5

Yes, they do.

🔊 **32**

Examiner:	Now you have about a minute to decide which idea would be best for the hotel.
Eva:	So, what do you think would be best for the hotel?
Paul:	I'd suggest either the swimming pool or the evening entertainment. Both those things are easy for people to see when they look on the website, and I think they would both be popular with guests.
Eva:	Well, I think everyone enjoys a swimming pool, especially children and young people. But on the other hand, most people only use a swimming pool in the summer, whereas evening entertainment can continue all year, and, like we said, they could offer different entertainment for different ages.
Paul:	That's true, so shall we choose the evening entertainment?
Eva:	Yes, let's go for that.

6 Pair 1 – C   Pair 2 – A   Pair 3 – B

🔊 **33**

Narrator:	Pair 1
Student 1:	Shall we talk about the swimming pool first? I think …
Student 2:	Yes, I think the swimming pool is a very good idea because most people enjoy …
Student 1:	I agree. Everyone loves swimming when the weather's hot, so …
Student 2:	But I don't think that tennis courts are a very good idea because most people …
Student 1:	But I think a lot of people like playing tennis!
Narrator:	Pair 2
Student 3:	I think that entertainment would be a great idea. Do you agree?
Student 4:	Yes. For example, there could be films for children to watch, and maybe shows later in the evening. Children always love watching films, especially with their friends, and I think older people like watching shows, like comedy shows, for example.
Student 3:	Yes, that's a good idea. Or maybe live music in the restaurant. I think that might be popular, because most restaurants don't have live music.
Student 4:	Yes. I think that entertainment would definitely attract more guests, especially if people don't have to pay for it. Not many hotels offer entertainment, do they?
Student 3:	No, so it would make this hotel a bit different, and I think people would choose it for that reason.
Student 4:	OK, shall we quickly talk about the other ideas?
Narrator:	Pair 3

Student 5:	Well, personally I think that reduced prices would be a very good idea because price is the most important thing for a lot of people. I also think that evening entertainment would be popular with guests, and that would attract people.
Student 6:	I would say that an award-winning chef would be a good idea, because it would improve the experience that people have in the hotel. I also think a swimming pool would attract more guests because most people enjoy swimming, especially in the summer.
Student 5:	But I don't believe that tennis courts would be very popular because only a small number of people play tennis, and they don't always want to play when they're on holiday.

7 1 b   2 e   3 a   4 c   5 d

🔊 **34**

Narrator:	1
Student 1:	It might be a good idea to offer reduced prices.
Narrator:	2
Student 2:	Perhaps they should have a swimming pool.
Narrator:	3
Student 1:	Tennis courts sound like a good idea.
Narrator:	4
Student 2:	They could offer entertainment for children, too.
Narrator:	5
Student 1:	I would say that an award-winning chef would be a good idea.

8 1 Do   2 do   3 Would   4 Do

🔊 **35**

Narrator:	1
Student 1:	Do you agree?
Narrator:	2
Student 2:	What do you think about the idea of a swimming pool?
Narrator:	3
Student 1:	Would you agree with that?
Narrator:	4
Student 2:	Do you think that's true?

9 1 think   2 that's   3 right   4 agree   5 mean; better
   6 sure   7 but

🔊 **36**

Narrator:	1
Student 1:	I think so, too.
Narrator:	2
Student 2:	Yes, that's true.
Narrator:	3
Student 1:	Yes, you're right.
Narrator:	4
Student 2:	I agree with you.
Narrator:	5
Student 1:	I can see what you mean, but I think a swimming pool might be a better idea.
Narrator:	6
Student 2:	I'm not sure about that.
Narrator:	7
Student 1:	Yes, that's true, but on the other hand, entertainment would also be popular.

10 a 2 and 4   b 5

🔊 37

Narrator: 1
Student 1: I'd suggest either the swimming pool or the evening entertainment.
Narrator: 2
Student 2: Are you OK with that?
Narrator: 3
Student 1: My choice would be the reduced prices.
Narrator: 4
Student 2: So, shall we choose the evening entertainment?
Narrator: 5
Student 1: Yes, let's go for that.

11

🔊 38

Examiner: Now, I'd like you to talk about something together for about two minutes. I'd like you to imagine that some people are discussing modern technology. Here are things that some people say it would be difficult to live without. Talk to each other about why it would be difficult to live without these things.
Student 1: Shall we start with the mobile phone? I definitely couldn't live without my phone, and I think most people would agree. What do you think?
Student 2: I agree. We use our phones for everything now – keeping in touch with friends, using the internet, finding information, taking photos. I think people depend on mobile phones more than they do on laptops, for example.
Student 1: I can see what you mean, but people use laptops for work, so they're also very important. People who travel for their jobs would find it very difficult to manage without a laptop.
Student 2: Yes, you're right. I hadn't thought about that. What do you think about a car? I think maybe people who live in cities could probably live without a car.
Student 1: Yes, that's true, although a car is much more important for people who live in the countryside. But most people live in cities, so a car is probably less important to them. I think people might find it very difficult to live without a bank card. Do you agree?
Student 2: Yes, I think so too. We're used to paying for everything with our cards, and it would be really annoying if we had to have money to pay for everything.
Student 1: Yes, that's true. On the other hand, we might spend less, which might be a good thing!
Student 2: Yes, maybe. …. I'm not sure about a washing machine. Do you think people could live without it?
Student 1: Well, it wouldn't be very convenient to be without a washing machine, but I think it would be OK. People could wash their clothes by hand. It would take more time than using a washing machine, but it would be possible.
Student 2: Yes, I think you're right.

12

🔊 39

Examiner: Now you have about a minute to decide which thing people would find it the most difficult to live without.

Student 1: So, which thing do you think people would find it the most difficult to live without?
Student 2: Well, for me it's definitely the bank card or the mobile phone. I think people use both these things a lot, and life would be very difficult without them. What do you think?
Student 1: Yes, I agree with you. I think the car and washing machine are nice to have, but I don't think people rely on them as much every day. And a laptop is important, but only for work, whereas a bank card and mobile phone are important for work and social life.
Student 2: Yes, that's true. Which would you choose between those two?
Student 1: Probably the phone, because I think people spend so much time on their phones, they would find it very difficult to be without it.
Student 2: OK, so shall we choose a mobile phone?
Student 1: Yes, let's go for that.

Part 4

3

Yes, they do.

4

B

🔊 40

Examiner: Alex, some people say that travel is bad for the environment. Do you agree?
Alex: Yes, I do, because I think that when people travel they use fuel, for example in a plane or a car, and that's very bad for the environment. They also create a lot of rubbish, for example if they have a picnic on the beach, and that's bad for the environment too.
Examiner: What do you think, Nicola?
Nicola: Well, I agree with Alex that travel can be bad for the environment, but on the other hand, I'd say that you can be a responsible tourist. For example, I prefer to travel by train because it's better for the environment, and I never leave rubbish. So I think it's possible to travel in a way that isn't bad for the environment.
Examiner: OK. Alex, what do you think young people can learn by going travelling?
Alex: Oh, I think they can learn a lot. For example, they can learn about other cultures and ways of life, and they can also see some of the problems that exist in other parts of the world. I think that travelling is very good for young people.
Examiner: What do you think about this, Nicola?
Nicola: I completely agree with Alex, and I also think that young people can benefit personally by becoming more independent when they go travelling. For example, when you're travelling you might have to deal with some difficult situations, and if you do this successfully, it can give you a lot of confidence.

5 Pair 1 – D   Pair 2 – A   Pair 3 – B

🔊 41

Narrator: Pair 1
Examiner: Tania, what places are popular for holidays in your country?

Tania:	Well, there are a lot of beaches in my country which are very popular for holidays, for local people and for people from other countries. There are also …
Peter:	Everyone wants to go to the beach in the summer! For example, in my country …
Narrator:	Pair 2
Examiner:	Bruno, what is the advantage of going on holiday with friends, rather than with family?
Bruno:	I think it's definitely more fun to go on holiday with your friends.
Examiner:	OK. Sofia, what do you think is the advantage of going on holiday with friends, rather than with family?
Sofia:	I agree with Bruno. I prefer to go on holiday with friends. I don't like going on holiday with my family.
Narrator:	Pair 3
Examiner:	Marina, some people say that tourism is bad for an area. What do you think?
Marina:	Well, I agree in some ways, because tourism can cause pollution and it can also make places very crowded. For example, if a beach is full of tourists, it isn't much fun for local people. But, on the other hand, tourism brings money into an area, and that's very good for it.
Examiner:	What do you think about this, Pablo?
Pablo:	Sorry, what did you say? Were you talking about tourism?

6 Student 1: Why?   Student 2: Where?   Student 3: When?

🔊 **42**

Narrator:	Student 1
Examiner:	Do you like eating in restaurants?
Nicola:	Yes, I really enjoy eating in restaurants. One reason is that I'm not a very good cook, so the food is much better in restaurants. Also, I think it's difficult to relax and enjoy food if you have to prepare it and then clean up afterwards. So, I prefer to eat in restaurants if I can.
Narrator:	Student 2
Examiner:	Do you think people should try to eat food that is produced locally?
Alex:	Yes, I think it's important to eat food that's produced locally. For example, where I live, the farmers grow a lot of different kinds of fruit and vegetables, and I think the people who live there should try to eat this food, to support the farmers.
Narrator:	Student 3
Examiner:	Some people think that advertising junk food should be banned on TV. Do you agree?
Bruno:	Well, junk food is obviously bad for people, especially children, and I definitely think that advertising it should be banned early in the evening, when children might be watching TV. For me, it isn't so bad later in the evening, because I don't think that advertising has such a big influence on adults.

8 Student 1 – Strategy 2   Student 2 – Strategy 1
   Student 3 – Strategy 3

🔊 **43**

Narrator:	Student 1
Examiner:	Which are the most popular sports in your country?

Peter:	Well, sport is very popular in my country, and a lot of people play sport or watch it on TV. I think the most popular sport is probably football because when there's a big match, for example if our national team is playing, nearly everybody watches the game.
Narrator:	Student 2
Examiner:	What could schools do to encourage healthy eating habits?
Tania:	Well, that's a very interesting question. Let me see. I would say that they could sell healthy snacks, and of course they could serve healthy food at lunchtime. Another thing is to teach children about why healthy food is important. I think schools should do all of these things.
Narrator:	Student 3
Examiner:	Is it better to exercise alone or with other people?
Sofia:	Well, on the one hand, I think maybe it's better to exercise alone if you are serious about getting fit, so you can really focus on your own fitness. But on the other hand, I think it's probably more fun to exercise with other people, in a class or in a team sport. So, I think this is probably better.

9

🔊 **44**

Examiner:	Some people say that there will be no shops in 20 years because people will buy everything online. Do you agree?
Alex:	Well, online shopping is definitely very popular nowadays, and a lot of people prefer it because it's quick, and it's often cheaper than buying things in a shop. Also, it's much easier to look on five different websites than to visit five different shops. But on the other hand, I think people will always want to see and touch some things before they buy them, especially if the things are expensive, so I think there will probably always be shops.
Examiner:	Are there advantages to living in the countryside rather than a big city?
Nicola:	Yes, I think there are some advantages to living in the countryside, especially for children. The countryside is safer than a city, so children can have more freedom to ride their bikes, for example. But I think that for teenagers and young adults the countryside is boring because there are no cinemas or concerts, or anything like that. So I'd prefer to be in a city.
Examiner:	Why do you think that so many people dream of becoming a celebrity?
Marina:	That's a good question. It's true that a lot of people, especially young people, would love to be a famous music star or sports star. I think they probably like the idea of being very rich and having a big house and expensive clothes. And they like the idea that everyone looks up to them. But I suspect they don't think about the disadvantages of being famous.
Examiner:	How do you think people benefit from going on holiday?
Pablo:	I think the main benefit is that you can relax on holiday and forget about work and exams, and all the things that are worrying you. Another big advantage is that you can travel to other places and see how people live there. I think that can help people to understand different cultures and think more about their own culture. For me, that's a big advantage of going on holiday.

Workbook answer key

UNIT 1
Listening
Part 3
Exam task
1 G   2 E   3 C   4 B   5 A

Grammar
1 1 I have   2 I'll call   3 You're going to be   4 I'm going
5 I'll be lying   6 I don't agree   7 I'm saving   8 love
9 I'm going to make   10 I'll fix

Vocabulary
1 1 off   2 after   3 out   4 with   5 on   6 to   7 in

Reading and Use of English
Part 5
1 1 writing letters, having a pen pal
2 a blog post
3 explaining the attractions of letter writing

Exam task
1 B   2 C   3 D

Vocabulary
1 1 become   2 highly   3 produce   4 greatly   5 turned
6 proved   7 play   8 deeply   9 involve   10 make
11 remain   12 widely

2 1 increase   2 extent   3 degree   4 percentage

Grammar
1 1 than   2 the   3 as   4 less   5 more   6 to   7 as   8 more
9 lot   10 less

Reading and Use of English
Part 1
Exam task
1 A   2 B   3 C   4 A   5 D   6 B   7 C   8 B

UNIT 2
Reading and Use of English
Part 6
1 an opinion article from a magazine/newspaper/website

Exam task
1 F   2 D   3 B   4 G   5 E   6 A

Listening
Part 1
1 1 monologue   2 dialogue   3 monologue   4 dialogue
5 dialogue   6 dialogue

Exam task
1 C   2 B   3 A   4 B   5 A   6 C

Grammar
1 1 used to
2 used to
3 used to / would
4 didn't use to
5 used to / would
6 used to
7 used to
8 used to

2 1 was
2 swam
3 have had
4 made
5 'd already formed
6 were sitting
7 've been
8 worked

3 1 steadily   temporarily   necessarily   extraordinarily
2 reasonably   preferably   suitably   considerably
3 actively   closely   alternatively   desperately
4 accidentally   gradually   mentally   potentially

4 1 considerably   2 extraordinarily   3 alternatively
4 mentally   5 closely   6 necessarily   7 reasonably
8 gradually

Vocabulary
1 1 exhausted   2 fascinating   3 thrilling   4 moved
5 relaxing   6 distressing   7 astonished   8 worrying

2 2 confusion   3 criticism   4 darkness
5 identification   6 journalism   7 laziness   8 partnership
9 racism   10 relationship   11 weakness   12 willingness

3 2 childless/childish   3 endless   4 foolish
5 harmful/harmless   6 hopeful/hopeless   7 mysterious
8 predictable   9 priceless   10 profitable   11 skilful
12 suspicious

4 1 confusion   2 suspicious   3 application   4 laziness
5 predictable   6 hopeless   7 priceless   8 identification
9 willingness   10 adventurous

Reading and Use of English
Part 3

Exam task

1 uncomfortable   2 breathtaking   3 surroundings   4 silently
5 peaceful   6 selection   7 service   8 educational

UNIT 3
Listening
Part 4

1 1 started, film club, because
2 What, difficult, beginning
3 What, like, teachers, to do
4 What, Alice's priority, club nights
5 running, club, Alice, pleasure from
6 What, Alice's attitude, teaching, how, write reviews
7 What advice, Alice give, starting, club

Exam task

1 A   2 B   3 A   4 C   5 C   6 B   7 A

Vocabulary

1 1 classical   2 rehearsals   3 guitarist   4 conductor
5 musicians   6 traditional   7 composer   8 recording

Reading and Use of English
Part 7

1 1 music/orchestras
2 Describing their experience of playing in an orchestra.
3 A violin, B flute, C trumpet, D violin

Exam task

1 B   2 A   3 C   4 D   5 B   6 C   7 A   8 D   9 A   10 C

Vocabulary

1 1 themes   2 entertaining   3 double act   4 script   5 cast
6 genre   7 series   8 soundtrack   9 plot   10 dialogue
11 release   12 special effects

2 1 released   2 genres   3 themes   4 series   5 cast
6 double act   7 entertaining   8 plot   9 script
10 dialogue   11 special effects   12 soundtrack

Grammar

1 1 f   2 c   3 g   4 a   5 h   6 b   7 e   8 d

2 1 will be bought
2 being opened
3 have been told
4 going to be cancelled
5 was being helped
6 are protected by

3 1 had her hair dyed
2 had a summer house built
3 to have photos taken
4 having my bike fixed

Reading and Use of English
Part 4

Exam task

1 get/have | your eyes
2 was | unaware of
3 haven't / have not seen | for / had not / hadn't seen | for
4 am/'m unlikely | to finish
5 aren't / are not | as many
6 shocked at | how

UNIT 4
Reading and Use of English
Part 5

1 1 Juventus
2 Liverpool Football Club
3 Manchester United's first female player of the year.

Exam task

1 B   2 A   3 C   4 D

Listening
Part 2

1 1 Yes. Sentences 1 and 2.
2 Yes. Sentence 4.
3 Sentence 2.
4 A verb: 4; adjectives: 3, 10; a noun or noun phrase: 1, 5, 6, 7, 8 and 9.

Exam task

1 having fun   2 5/five   3 gentle   4 ride a bike   5 seal
6 reflections   7 yoga   8 motor   9 backpack   10 windy

Vocabulary

1 1 injury   2 X-ray   3 surgery   4 swollen   5 recovery
6 heal   7 therapy   8 bruise   9 strained   10 aching

2 1 reaction   2 poisonous   3 medical   4 sensation
5 examination   6 physically   7 suffering   8 psychological

3 1 on   2 at   3 in   4 in   5 at   6 On

Grammar

1 1 must have
2 was able to
3 should have checked
4 might have left
5 haven't been able
6 must remember to
7 don't need
8 can't have been

2
1 may not see
2 should have booked
3 mustn't forget
4 can't spend
5 might not let
6 have to practise
7 should have been
8 don't need to / needn't give
9 must have forgotten
10 don't have to go

3 1 on   2 at   3 in   4 in   5 at   6 On

Reading and Use of English
Part 2

1 1 which   2 as   3 instead   4 such   5 apart   6 but
7 mine   8 up

Exam task
1 round/around
2 there
3 who/that
4 most
5 least
6 although/while/whilst
7 matter
8 without

UNIT 5
Listening
Part 2

Exam task
1 bathroom
2 bridge weekend
3 9/nine
4 electronic art
5 virtual reality
6 puzzle
7 informal
8 smart home device
9 data scientists
10 email

Reading and Use of English
Part 7

2 Mentioned: 1, 2, 3, 4, 5, 7
Not effective: 2, 4

Exam task
1 B   2 A   3 D   4 C   5 B   6 C   7 B   8 D   9 A   10 C

Vocabulary
1 1 went   2 get   3 get   4 gone   5 get   6 got   7 go   8 go

2 1 on   2 through   3 away   4 for   5 across   6 off   7 by

Grammar
1 1 shouldn't
2 doing
3 had been
4 hadn't broken
5 weren't
6 knew

2 1 had got
2 had remembered
3 met
4 was/were
5 didn't play
6 would let
7 hadn't tripped up
8 worked
9 didn't have to
10 had worn

3 1 if you don't
2 long as you manage to
3 could only go home early / could go home early only
4 wouldn't have had
5 can't help because
6 in case you
7 be impossible unless
8 wish I hadn't told

Reading and Use of English
Part 1

Exam task
1 B   2 D   3 C   4 A   5 C   6 D   7 A   8 C

UNIT 6
Listening
Part 4

2 Question 4.

Exam task
1 C   2 A   3 C   4 A   5 B   6 B   7 A

Vocabulary
1 A 4   B 3   C 5   D 2   E 1

1 transparent   2 generate   3 gases   4 recycled   5 quality
6 pollute   7 renewable   8 harmful

Grammar

1 1 The book wasn't ~~enough~~ interesting **enough** so I stopped reading it.

2 It's a long way and we are ~~so~~ **too** tired to walk.

3 I wanted to look at the view but the window was ~~to~~ **too** dirty.

4 The exam was hard because ~~time wasn't enough~~ **there wasn't enough time** to finish it.

5 If we go for a swim today we'll be ~~so~~ **too** cold to enjoy it.

6 This cookbook is good because the instructions aren't ~~hard enough~~ **too hard**.

2 1 so   2 such   3 so   4 such   5 such   6 so

Reading and Use of English
Part 2

Exam task

1 As   2 there   3 so   4 unless   5 which   6 if/though
7 from   8 until

Reading and Use of English
Part 6

Exam task

1 G   2 E   3 B   4 A   5 F   6 C

Grammar

1 1 lifestyles
2 pressure
3 experience
4 misunderstanding
5 impressions
6 rubbish
7 arguments
8 research
9 evidence
10 breakthroughs

2 1 I watched **the** most amazing documentary about Namibia at **the** weekend.

2 My mum used to be **an** actor and she still loves going to **the** theatre as often as she can.

3 My brother's in hospital because he broke his leg playing in **a** football match.

4 **The** Bengal tiger is native to **the** Indian subcontinent and is threatened with extinction.

5 My family and I have just had **a** wonderful summer holiday in **the** Alps.

6 Scientists have been trying to warn governments for many years about **the** dangers of global warming.

7 Why don't you come round to my house after dinner tonight, and we can choose **a** film to watch?

8 I'd love to go to **a** concert with you in **the** summer. I love listening to live music.

UNIT 7
Listening
Part 3

Exam task

1 C   2 H   3 F   4 D   5 A

Grammar

1 1 to change
2 living
3 to win
4 to be
5 discussing
6 asking
7 to speak
8 to pay
9 to finish
10 providing
11 to forget
12 to give

2a 1 how big his business was.

2 if he would carry on doing this (running his business) when he was an adult.

3 if there was anything he regretted about starting a business.

4 if he had any advice for other young entrepreneurs / what advice he had for other young entrepreneurs.

2b A 3   B 4   C 2   D 1

2c 1 was; would
2 wouldn't
3 couldn't / wasn't able to
4 let; couldn't

3 1 My sister begged me to go to the party with her.

2 The teacher stressed how important it was for us to finish / the importance of us finishing the work by Tuesday.

3 The salesman assured me that the skateboard was the best I could get within my budget.

4 My brother rejected the idea of getting Mum flowers for her birthday.

5 Dad defended his decision to buy the coat.

6 Mary swore she'd be there by eight. / Mary swore to be there by eight.

7 My sister declared that she was going on a solo 60-kilometre bike ride the next/following day.

8 Mum checked that I had remembered my dental appointment.

Reading and Use of English
Part 4

Exam task
1 gave up | running
2 to know | if I was
3 was not / wasn't | nearly as
4 'd/would have | bought
5 never been to | such
6 disappointing when | I am / I'm given

Vocabulary

1 1 brand   2 fault   3 competitive   4 exchanged
5 appeared   6 browsing   7 launch   8 consumers
9 bargains   10 purchase   11 stock   12 offer

2

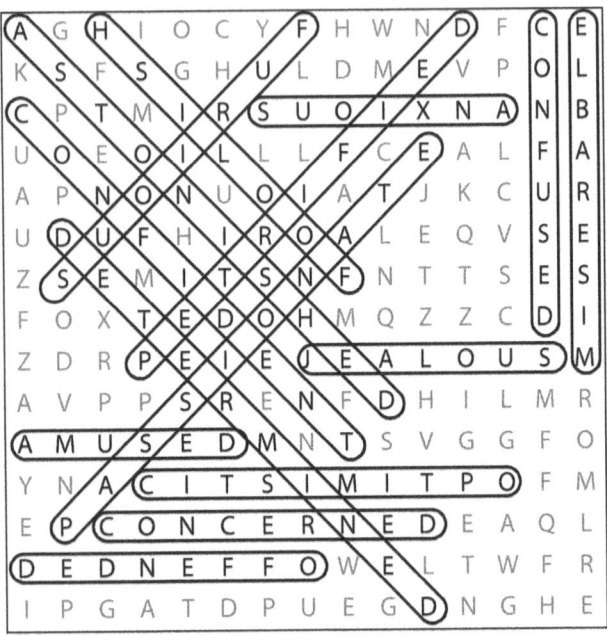

1 AMUSED   2 ASTONISHED   3 CONFUSED
4 FURIOUS   5 ANXIOUS   6 FOOLISH   7 MISERABLE
8 PASSIONATE   9 JEALOUS   10 CONFIDENT   11 OPTIMISTIC
12 PETRIFIED   13 CONCERNED   14 DETERMINED
15 OFFENDED

Writing

1 C, A, B

2 1 C   2 B   3 A

3 1 It's not worth wasting your time here. (expressing personal opinion)
2 I strongly recommend that you go. (making recommendations)
3 It was alright on the whole. (expressing personal opinion)
4 The staff are very helpful. (giving a factual description)
5 It sells a good range of shoes at reasonable prices. (giving a factual description)

6 There are two floors, and everything is clearly signposted. (giving a factual description)
7 The changing rooms are small and badly lit. (giving a factual description)
8 I feel that the place has been well designed. (expressing personal opinion)

4 1 well   2 absolutely   3 incredibly   4 completely
5 brilliantly   6 extraordinarily

5 We are looking for reviews of local department stores. Your review should include information about <u>where the department store is</u>, <u>what sort of things it sells</u> and <u>what the staff are like</u>. Would you recommend the department store to other young shoppers?

Exam task
Model answer
<u>Greens Department Store</u>
Greens Department Store is in the main square of my town, opposite the fountain. It's one of my favourite places to visit when I go into the town centre. The shop has three floors and sells everything you can think of, from clothes and shoes, to furniture, cards and sports equipment. My younger brother especially loves the toy department, which has an excellent selection of good-quality toys.
One thing I love about Greens is that the staff are so friendly and knowledgeable. Last time I went, my dad was looking for a new suit for a wedding. The assistants were amazingly helpful and we left the shop with the perfect suit.
I would recommend anyone visiting my town to go to Greens. Even if you don't need to do any shopping, you will have fun browsing the different departments. And, of course, it's the perfect place to have lunch. Greens has a superb café, serving delicious hot and cold food.

UNIT 8
Reading and Use of English
Part 3

1 unacceptable   unaware   inconvenient   decorative
desirable   doubtful/doubtless   endless   extensive
harmful/harmless   illegal   impatient   impolite
preferable   skilful   invisible   unwilling

2 advice   belief   growth   height   length   proof
pride   sight   strength   width

3 automatically   admittedly   (un)comfortably
continually/continuously   dramatically   (un)enthusiastically
unexpectedly   financially   (un)happily   (un)necessarily
passionately   primarily   readily   (un)scientifically
(un)successfully   (un)surprisingly   suspiciously

Exam task
1 closely   2 instructions   3 satisfaction   4 increasingly
5 effective   6 discovery   7 presence   8 impossible

Listening

Part 1

Exam task
1 C   2 B   3 A   4 B   5 B   6 C   7 A   8 B

Vocabulary

1
1 software engineer, g
2 hard drive, e
3 computer operator, b
4 virtual reality, h
5 social networking, c
6 search engine, a
7 message board, f
8 internet access, d

2 2 bookmark   3 download   4 broadband   5 database
6 spreadsheet   7 undo   8 input

3 1 satellite   2 microphone   3 laser   4 telescope
5 thermometer   6 monitor

Grammar

1 1 b   2 c   3 i   4 f   5 j   6 h   7 d   8 a   9 g   10 e

2 2, 3, 4, 5, 9

3 2 The NASA website, which I love, is updated regularly.
3 Chris Hadfield, who is famous for playing the guitar on the space station, spent 166 days in space.
4 The international space station, where many science experiments are done, is 420 kilometres above the Earth.
5 The photos of space on the NASA website, which are very colourful, are amazing.
6 There's a podcast, which I plan to listen to, about the history of space.
7 The international space station, which requires a crew of seven, has housed astronauts since 2000.

Writing

1 You must include three points – two that you are given and one of your own.

2 The writer agrees with the statement. The writer's own idea is 'online shopping'.

3 1 However   2 For example   3 If   4 Instead of
5 As a result   6 Another way   7 Although

4 There is no conclusion. Everything else is there.

5 A is the best conclusion because the ideas in it relate to the rest of the essay, i.e. that the internet is in fact making us lazy. B is positive about the internet in a way that does not match the rest of the essay.

6 Ideas for 'your own idea': travel / news / social life / communication

Model answer
It's hard to imagine life without the internet. Although it's true that the internet takes a lot of effort out of things that used to be difficult, such as going to a library to look up information, this does not mean it's making us lazy, in my opinion.
If we consider entertainment on the internet, people say that streaming services allow us to sit around watching shows all day instead of being active. However, think about how many young people make videos to share online. Often, these involve a lot of creativity and effort.
The internet can be used to keep in touch with friends without leaving your home, which some say is lazy. However, most people socialise in person as well, so I strongly disagree with this.
Finally, think about how the internet encourages us to travel. We see all these wonderful places online and then make plans to get up off the sofa and actually go there ourselves. Therefore, I would argue that even though the internet allows us to do things at home that in the past required more physical effort, in many ways the internet actually encourages us not to be lazy.

VOCABULARY EXTRA

Unit 1

1 Across   2 carnival   3 parade   4 gather   5 costume
7 decoration
Down   1 tradition   6 reception

2 1 stick   2 break   3 cheat   4 look   5 make   6 keep
7 pick   8 broke   9 rely   10 put

3 1 bond   2 circle   3 tension   4 upbringing   5 introductions
6 separation

Unit 2

1 1 last   2 voyage   3 connection   4 sight   5 territory

2 1 see   2 stopped   3 keep   4 pull   5 get   6 catch
7 headed   8 turn   9 made

3 1 inner city   2 outskirts   3 community spirit   4 picturesque
5 housing estate   6 suburb   7 public spaces   8 residential

Unit 3

1 1 make out   2 sold out   3 stood out   4 soaking up
5 identified with   6 get across

2a 2 C   3 B   4 F   5 D   6 A

2b 1 appearances   2 promote   3 crew   4 location
5 streaming   6 approval   7 outline   8 edits   9 publicity

3 1 choir   2 goes   3 beat/rhythm   4 charts   5 track/solo
6 lyrics   7 solo   8 rhythm

Unit 4

1 competitive sports
football pitch
represent your country
save a goal
set a record
shoot at a target
victory lap
win the trophy

2 1 save; goal
2 set; record
3 victory lap
4 represent your country
5 football pitch
6 shoot; at a target
7 competitive sports
8 won the trophy

3 1 condition e
2 eyesight f
3 pharmacist a
4 remedy g
5 sneeze d
6 symptom b
7 vitamin c
8 wound h

4 2 *peel* is the odd word out. The rest are to do with eating food.
3 *sour* is the odd word out. The rest are types of food.
4 *starving* is the odd word out. The rest describe how food tastes.
5 *pudding* is the odd word out. The rest all relate to bread.
6 *ripe* is the odd word out. The rest all describe food that is past its best.

Unit 5

1 1 an idea
2 an opportunity
3 a chance
4 in concentration
5 an error

2 1 for   2 from   3 in   4 to   5 beyond   6 in   7 from   8 to
9 of   10 to

3 1 learning   2 educated   3 discipline   4 standards
5 rejected   6 training   7 sitting   8 study

Unit 6

1 1 organic   2 earthquake   3 stormy   4 tropical   5 reserve
6 footprint   7 chemicals   8 green   9 ground
10 Conservation
The word in grey is atmosphere.

2 1 endangered   2 ecological   3 extinction   4 coastal
5 environmental   6 globally   7 regional   8 renewable
9 biological

3 1 bark   2 feathers   3 territory   4 trap   5 paw   6 leopard
7 swan   8 wasp   9 owl   10 habitat

Unit 7

1a 1 certainty   2 despair/desperation   3 dissatisfaction
4 impatience   5 passion   6 relief   7 suspicion
8 sympathy

1b 1 impatience   2 sympathy   3 passion   4 desperation
5 certainty   6 relief   7 Dissatisfaction   8 suspicion

2 1 nerves   2 ears   3 breath   4 spirits   5 mood   6 heart
7 face   8 temper   9 fool   10 death

3 1 b   2 d   3 f   4 e   5 a   6 c

Unit 8

1 1 evidence   2 study   3 statistics   4 observations
5 breakthrough   6 theory   7 discovery   8 cure
9 scale   10 progress

2 1 A   2 C   3 B   4 A   5 B   6 A

3 1 performed   2 thought of   3 made clear
4 were discovered   5 constitute   6 proposed

Workbook audio scripts

🔊 02 **Unit 1, Listening Part 3**

You will hear five short extracts in which teenagers are talking about making new friends. For questions 1–5, choose from the list (A–H) what each speaker says. Use the letters only once. There are three extra letters which you do not need to use.

Speaker 1

I've had lots of practice at making new friends! Because of my dad's job, we had to move to a new city every two years. It was tough, I'm not going to pretend it wasn't. Those first days at a new school I was always nervous. But luckily, I'm an outgoing person and I enjoy building up a new social circle. One thing to realise though – the worst thing you can do is try to rush things. Just be patient – let the process take its course. Also, remember that people will always be curious about someone new. Don't take offence at annoying questions – just smile, and be polite.

Speaker 2

When I was little, it was so easy to make a new friend. I just went up to someone I liked and said, 'Do you want to be my friend?' Nine times out of ten, they said yes and off we went! Once you get to secondary school it doesn't work quite like that. In that environment you need to act cool – give the impression that you're completely at ease, no matter what's going on inside. That way, people will find you interesting and want to learn more about you. You'll get asked to do stuff with them outside school and from there you'll be friends in no time.

Speaker 3

I think making new friends is quite hard. I know there are people who can just strike up a conversation with a stranger, and straight away they're laughing and joking together, as if they've known each other for years. But for the rest of us it takes a bit more effort. If I find myself chatting to someone that I'd like to be better friends with, I'll try and point out something I know we both enjoy – it might be a sport we both do, or the fact that we're both good at art, that sort of thing. A shared love of something is the root of a good friendship, I think.

Speaker 4

The temptation when you're trying to make new friends is to really go for it – make loads of jokes, get everyone laughing, generally make yourself seem as interesting as possible. This can have the opposite effect to the one you're after, though. What you want to do is let people see the true you. Answer questions honestly and be as natural as you can. Joining clubs is quite a good thing to do, too. Sometimes it's easier to talk when you're both busy doing something – it gets rid of those awkward silences, which can be really uncomfortable.

Speaker 5

One thing that separates an acquaintance from a friend is that as well as having fun together, friends support each other through the tough times. Offering to be there for someone is a great way to build a stronger relationship. It doesn't have to be anything emotional – it could just be that you are both entered into a race, for example, and you have some good tips on how to train and what you should be eating. The thought of doing this might make you feel a bit nervous, but it really shouldn't.

🔊 03 **Unit 2, Listening Part 1**

You will hear people talking in six different situations. For questions 1–6, choose the best answer (A, B or C).

1 *You hear a boy talking about a computer course he did during his summer holiday.*

Boy: My dad found out about it, and he booked me onto it. I'm not sure how he heard about it. He's really keen for me not to waste my time during the holidays. I try to explain to him, and Mum does too, that it's OK to chill out a bit once in a while, but he's not having it. I wasn't against the idea, to be fair, even though it did eat into my free time quite a bit. But I picked up a lot of stuff that I didn't know, and the tutors managed to make it challenging and interactive.

2 *You hear two friends talking about a podcast series.*

Friend 1: Thanks for telling me about that podcast series. I listened to an episode last night and it was just as funny as you said it would be.

Friend 2: They're great, those presenters, aren't they? It doesn't matter what they're talking about – I just love the way they are together.

Friend 1: The episode I chose was the history of biscuits. I'm not sure how much time they actually spoke about that, though!

Friend 2: Not much, I imagine! Try the one on ballpoint pens. Honestly, you won't regret it!

Friend 1: If you say so!

3 *You hear a report on the radio about an expedition.*

Reporter: This month a team of adventurers from Britain will first climb, and then cycle down one of the world's highest mountains. Exactly which one is yet to be revealed, but it will be over 7,000 metres high. The idea is to raise money for community projects that enable young people aged from 12 to 18 to get involved in adventurous sport. You can support the project by visiting the expedition website and donating online. You can also find biographies of the adventurers and technical details about all their gear.

4 *You hear a girl talking to her father about a problem she's got.*

Girl: I asked a teacher about borrowing a laptop, Dad, but none are available.

Dad: Well, you'll have to carry on using mine for the moment.

Girl: Yours is so old and slow. What did the guy at the repair shop say about mine?

Dad: He still hasn't got back to me, actually.

Girl: But it's been two weeks. Surely they've had time to look at it by now?

Dad: I'll pop in tomorrow after work and see what I can find out.

Girl: I bet they'll say it needs replacing. We should have got a new one as soon as it broke!

5 *You hear a teenager talking to his grandmother about his recent move.*

Gran: How are you settling in to your new home, Tom? What do you think of the town?

Tom: It's interesting, Gran, nothing like where we were before. Not as many people of course – but everything we need is right here. I mean school, the doctor, the shops, the train station. Honestly, it takes no more than ten minutes from our house to get to all those. There are lots of cycle paths as well, so getting around is a piece of cake. I miss my friends though, and the places we used to go to together. It doesn't quite feel like home yet.

Gran: Early days! You've not been there very long.

6 *You hear part of a class debate.*

Speaker 1: OK, what a great debate we're having! It's fantastic to get all your views on the new statue they are putting up in our town square. Now, does anyone want to add anything? Oh yes – Julie. Go ahead, what would you like to say?

Julie: I honestly don't see what everyone is going on about. We want more tourists to visit our town, don't we? Well, in that case we've got to make improvements. The square was so bare and boring before. Fair enough, this statue might not be to everyone's taste, but you're never going to please everyone.

🔊 **04** Unit 3, Listening Part 4

You will hear an interview with a teenager called Alice Fields, who runs a film club at her school. For questions 1–7, choose the best answer (A, B or C).

Interviewer: My guest today is Alice Fields, a student at Treeway High School. Last year Alice started a film club for students at her school and it's been a huge success. In fact, two members have won national awards for film reviews they've written. Alice, tell us what inspired you to start your club?

Alice: Well, I'm obsessed with films – I want to work in the film industry when I'm older. But when I chatted to my friends about it, none of them seemed to get it. I felt they were missing out, so I just thought – how can I get them to have the same enthusiasm for it that I have? And starting a film club seemed one way to do that.

Interviewer: And how did you go about setting up the club?

Alice: Well, I had to see if the Head Teacher would let me do it first. Students don't normally run clubs at my school so there was no set procedure. Initially it was 'Oh no, that's so complicated! We don't know what to do about that!' But I stuck at it, and eventually they agreed. Then I persuaded a friend to help me get it going. We did some advertising around the school and slowly but surely students started to sign up.

Interviewer: And how much staff involvement is there now?

Alice: We have a teacher who observes, but that's it – the running of the club is down to us. But hardly a week goes by when a teacher doesn't drop in to see what we're watching or have a chat with me about a film I've advertised on a club poster. In fact, I'm now looking into opening up the club to staff as well as pupils – I've got a feeling there's enough interest.

Interviewer: Tell me what happens on a typical club night.

Alice: Well, we watch the film of course, and then we either have a follow-up discussion on the themes, or I run a session on review writing. But the main thing is the film. I want to get that sense of being in a cinema. I set out the seats in rows, I bring popcorn, I show trailers, all that! But I do expect people to behave well. I have rules on what's acceptable and what's not, and I remind people of them when needed.

Interviewer: What do you enjoy about running your film club?

Alice: So many things! One is witnessing friendships grow between people who had previously never spoken to each other. It doesn't seem to matter if one is 11 and the other is 14 – as soon as they realise they both love the same type of film, they've got that thing in common with each other and they never look back.

Interviewer: Now, what about those members of yours who won awards for their film reviews? How do you teach them to write good reviews?

Alice: So, when I coach the club on writing reviews, I talk a lot about the six essential elements of film: the three Cs, which are: colour, camera, character, and the three Ss, which are: story, setting, and sound. I remind students to think about these elements in turn and that usually prompts ideas. I also tell them not to be afraid to say things that lots of people will disagree with. After all, you've got to grab the reader's attention somehow.

Interviewer: And finally, what advice would you give to someone thinking of starting up a film club of their own?

Alice: Oh – go for it! The benefits are huge, honestly – but do be prepared for the hard work! Things to bear in mind – stick to the same day and time every week, otherwise attendance will drop. Assign roles to students as this encourages a sense of ownership. Also – don't have an age barrier, and finally avoid putting any pressure on people to go each week. Just let them dip in and out as they please.

Interviewer: Fantastic! Thanks, Alice …

🔊 **05** Unit 4, Listening Part 2

You will hear a teenager called Louise Porter giving a class presentation about a water sport called paddle boarding. For questions 1–10, complete the sentences with a word or short phrase.

Louise: Morning, everyone! In my presentation today I'm going to talk about my favourite sport – paddle boarding. It's a sport that has its roots in surfing. To do it, you stand up on a board that floats on the water, and move yourself along using a long stick with a broad, flat end, called a paddle.

The idea of standing on a board and using a stick to move yourself along isn't new, of course. When I was doing my research for this presentation, I found out that for thousands of years, cultures from Africa, South America and Asia did this for the purposes of fishing, travelling and even, surprisingly, having fun, which I thought was brilliant!

In its modern form, paddle boarding's been part of the water sports scene for about 20 years, but its popularity really took off about five years ago. My family and I first tried it two years ago and I can tell you it's currently the world's fastest-growing sport.

It's not hard to see why. For one thing, paddle boarding's a great way to get fit. You have to use all your major muscle groups, and it gives your heart and lungs a workout, but at the same time it's quite gentle. This suits people who for whatever reason aren't into tough, energetic workouts.

What it's also got going for it is that it is so straightforward to learn – nothing like as hard as learning to ride a bike, for example. One thing I'd say though, is that it's really important to learn how to swim before you go paddle boarding, if you can't do it already.

Another attraction of paddle boarding is that it lets you get really close to nature. We paddle board in the sea near our home, and there's so much wildlife to see. I've always got my eyes open in case I spot a dolphin or a porpoise, and just last weekend a seal jumped onto my paddle board. It gave me such a fright! But it soon realised my board wasn't a rock after all, and slipped back into the water.

I love paddle boarding on rivers too. You can see a lot more from a paddle board than from, say, a canoe or a kayak. You're standing up, for one thing, so you have a much better view. Also, you can look down into the water from a paddle board. From a kayak, the reflections usually make that impossible.

What's great about paddle boarding is that it's so easy to mix with other activities. My mum does yoga on hers – it sounds crazy, but I'm going to have a go soon, and I can't wait. For my dad, it's all about using the board to go birdwatching. I go with him now and again and it's quite fun – but perhaps a bit too slow and quiet for me.

To make it easier to do different things on your paddle board, it's possible these days to get a board that you can attach things to, such as a picnic box, or a chair. I've seen some that you can add a motor to, but for me, that's going a step too far!

When it comes to buying a paddle board, there are so many types available, depending on what you are going to use it for. Ours are the inflatable kind that you blow up using a pump. The great thing about these, compared to solid ones, is that they fit in a backpack and you can carry them easily. You don't need a special rack on the car or anything like that.

You must be wondering if there are any negatives at all to this sport. Well, not many, actually! We go out onto the water all year round, even in the winter, when it's freezing cold. The only thing that puts me off is if it's a really windy day. But other than that, we make sure we have the right clothes and equipment and just get on with it!

🔊 06 **Unit 5, Listening Part 2**

You will hear a man called Paul Mathers talking about a summer technology camp for teenagers. For questions 1–10, complete the sentences with a word or short phrase.

Paul: Hello, everyone! My name's Paul and it's great to see so many of you here for my talk. As you know, I'm going to tell you all about Teencoders summer camps. These are a fun way to learn computer programming through projects such as 3D game design, laser printing and loads more. It's a fascinating topic and one that's so important in our modern world.

Our courses run throughout August, and are held at a beautiful location called Helmsely College. Accommodation is in single bedrooms and there's one bathroom for every four students. Our residential campers usually stay for a week. They arrive on Sunday night and leave on Friday afternoon. People who live nearby can come as a day camper.

For students who wish to stay for longer, we offer something we call a 'bridge weekend'. It's very reasonably priced and covers food, accommodation and fun activities, including a cinema trip, from Friday afternoon until the new campers arrive on Sunday evening.

So let me tell you about the daily schedule. Campers wake up around 8.00 a.m. and breakfast is available between 8.15 and 8.45. Day campers are expected to turn up no later than 9.00, ready for everyone to start sessions at 9.30. Typically, there are five sessions a day with an hour-long break for lunch at 1.00. The sessions end at 5.30.

After dinner, residential campers choose from a range of evening activities, such as laser tag, or chocolate making. This year for the first time we're adding electronic art to that list, so it'll be interesting to see how popular that is. Campers can also choose to play board games or use the time for relaxation.

So, what are some of the things you can learn on this course? Well, as you know, the tech world moves incredibly quickly, and we make a huge effort to keep up. Virtual reality has come on massively over the past few years, so that features in our courses, but of course we also cover basic programming principles. You won't get far without that.

For the first hour of the day, we present students with a puzzle. We find this gets people's brains into the right place for the rest of the day's learning, and also helps settle everyone down. Students love it and say the time flies by much quicker than it does in a normal lesson.

After that there's a morning lecture. We call it that, but that makes it sound terribly serious. In fact, groups are small enough that everyone can ask questions whenever they like. It's very informal but lots of new material is presented so concentration is essential.

In the afternoons, you get to put what you have learnt into practice. For instance, we might get you to design a smart home device. Actually doing stuff is a great way of learning. Reading about how someone else designed a video game, for example, just won't be as effective.

Our tutors are all amazing and the teenagers who come on our courses rate them very highly indeed. We employ university students who are all aiming for careers in technology. Some of our former tutors are data scientists now, and sometimes we invite them in to run sessions on technology careers.

So, we really hope to see you at a camp soon. Have a word with your parents tonight. They needn't worry about you. We promise to send them email updates every day on your activities and progress. It's a great way to keep in touch as we don't allow mobile phones on the course!

You will hear an interview with a young blogger called Emma, who's talking about living a 'zero-waste' life. For questions 1–7, choose the best answer (A, B or C).

Interviewer: Hello, everyone and welcome to this week's podcast. I'm very pleased to have with me in the studio today teen blogger Emma Jackson. Emma, tell us a bit about zero-waste blogging.

Emma: Well, it's really catching on! Some people who do it have become really famous. For those who don't know, the zero-waste movement's all about cutting the amount of waste you produce to an absolute minimum. The most famous zero-waste bloggers, the ones who started the whole thing off, produce just a jam jar's worth of waste a year, which really is quite incredible! I admire them, but that's not possible for me. I just try to live, as far as possible, without generating too much rubbish.

Interviewer: I know some people have a problem with the term zero-waste. What about you?

Emma: It's something we're stuck with, I think. But it does give people who disagree with us something to attack with, which is unfortunate. I've read loads of articles saying that because we do throw some stuff away, we are cheats and liars. If we could say we're low-wasters for example, that would solve a lot of problems. And, of course, no one can ever actually get to 100 percent zero waste, so it's not the most accurate way of describing what we do.

Interviewer: So, Emma, have you always had a good attitude towards waste?

Emma: I'm afraid not! It's been a slow process. My dad has always been really into environmental issues and nature and all that, and you'd think this would have influenced me – and I guess it did have an effect eventually, given what I do now. But when I was little and my parents tried to get me to put rubbish in the right recycling bin, I really couldn't be bothered.

Interviewer: Like all of us, I guess! Now I've heard about a neighbourhood survey you did. Tell me about that.

Emma: It was something we did for our geography class. We had to write a survey, and go out and collect information on our neighbours' recycling habits and how they felt about waste, that kind of thing. It really opened my eyes to just how much stuff we throw away unnecessarily and I slowly started to think about my own behaviour.

Interviewer: So, what was the first thing you did?

Emma: I stopped using plastic drinking straws. It's not something that's going to change the world, I know that, and it's kind of embarrassing to say really, now that I have gone so much further. But it got me onto the right track mentally, to go on and do bigger things. Gradually, after that, I did more; I became aware of people on social media, read some really inspiring stories, and it just flowed from there really.

Interviewer: So, give us some tips. What would you say to someone who's just starting out?

Emma: Well, it's funny, people start trying to live a zero-waste life and they look around their home and all they can see is plastic stuff – toothbrushes, hair brushes, clothes hangers, you name it. The temptation is to immediately throw out all this perfectly good stuff and go out and get eco-friendly ones made of wood or metal. That's not a good idea though – make sure you use whatever you have until it comes to the end of its life. Then by all means, get the eco-catalogue out and treat yourself!

Interviewer: That's great advice, Emma. I'm sure there are lots of mistakes people make. Any last words of advice on that?

Emma: Yes, be realistic. Mistakes are fine, accidents are normal. I've been known to go out on a hot day without my reusable water bottle and then I have to get a plastic bottle of water from a store. Or I leave my fabric napkin at home and need to use paper ones. I am angry with myself, sure, and I try not to do it too often. But none of us are perfect, we're just humans trying to do our best. That's how I look at it.

You will hear five short extracts in which teenagers are talking about going shopping. For questions 1–5, choose from the list (A–H) what each speaker says about going shopping with friends. Use the letters only once. There are three extra letters which you do not need to use.

Speaker 1

Not everybody likes going clothes shopping with friends. Some people find the whole thing a real bore and just want to get into the shop and out of it as fast as they can. For me, it depends a lot on what I want to buy. If it's something fairly routine like a pair of jeans, I'm happy to have company. I know I'm not going to hold people up, or drive them crazy with my inability to make a decision. But if I'm feeling adventurous and want to explore shops I've never been to, then I'd rather do that by myself.

Speaker 2

I definitely prefer shopping with friends to shopping alone, especially if I need something quite urgently. On my own, I seem to get distracted really easily – I might need a top for a party that evening for example, and yet somehow I find myself wandering around shoe shops, or looking at sportswear. And the other thing is mistakes – friends have stopped me more than once from buying something on impulse that I would most likely have regretted, and then had to return. I'm not saying I always listen to what they say, I do have my own opinions too, but often I'm glad they were there!

Speaker 3

I love clothes shopping, but at the moment I'm on a tight budget – I'm saving up for a new skateboard, so I'm not buying new stuff. I do still go shopping with my mates though. It's an important part of how we socialise. We have a lot of fun, trying on different things, discussing the latest trends and giving each other advice. Shopping together brings us closer as a group for sure. It's interesting because we all have different styles, so it's surprising that it works so well. I guess we're in tune with each other's tastes, so we naturally take that into account when we give each other advice.

Speaker 4

Most of the time I shop alone. I seem to get more done in a shorter amount of time. But my best friend Holly and I are good shopping partners. We don't get impatient if one of us takes forever in a particular store – but at the same time we don't drag the other one into stores we know they hate. I love shopping for jewellery, for example, but Holly hates it. So while I do that she might spend time looking at make-up, or just have a coffee. I've got several friends I refuse to go shopping with – it sounds awful but I'd just rather go by myself.

Speaker 5

If you're the type of person that's really confident about their style, then you probably don't need anyone else's input, and you probably don't need to go shopping with other people. But if you're like me, someone who appreciates a bit of support and advice, then you will. I suppose you could ask the shop assistant, but when it's a friend, you trust that person and they know you and your tastes well. My friends often come up with ideas for outfits that would never occur to me. They open my eyes to possibilities that I wouldn't see otherwise.

🔊 **09** **Unit 8, Listening Part 1**

You will hear people talking in eight different situations. For questions 1–8, choose the best answer (A, B or C).

1 *You hear two students talking about a school project.*

Boy: The geography project sounds like it's going to be a lot of work, doesn't it?

Girl: It really does! But at least the teacher's given us a couple of months to do it. That takes the pressure off a bit. I just wish we didn't have to do it with a partner – I get on much better on my own.

Boy: You are funny! I don't mind that, but I wasn't sure about the topic. Is there that much to say about flooding?

Girl: Well, yeah. It's getting to be a real problem in some parts of the world, isn't it?

2 *You hear a young person talking about his work.*

My grandma looked after me a lot when I was growing up because my parents worked long hours. She taught me to bake, and my favourite thing to make was cupcakes. It was when I was about 15 that I started selling them, and the business just grew from there. Now I'm 18 and I've got employees, my own factory … I'm not quite sure how it happened. It's not what I imagined I'd be doing as a career but I've got no plans to stop just yet. In the long term though, I imagine I will move on to something else.

3 *You hear two friends talking about a display of winter lights in their local park.*

Boy: I went to see the lights in the park last night.

Girl: Oh, what did you think of them? I haven't been, as Mum says the ticket price is ridiculous.

Boy: It is, to be honest. I mean, it does look amazing – there are lights through all the trees, along the paths and on the buildings. But the whole thing is over in 30 minutes and you're not given a chance to really appreciate it – there are staff all along the route encouraging you to keep moving.

Girl: I'd hate that. Is it because there are lots of people there?

Boy: I've heard it can get crowded, but it wasn't when we were there.

4 *You hear a critic talking about a film.*

I wasn't expecting much when I went to see this one – the reviews that have come out in the press so far didn't fill me with confidence. But I adored it. It almost felt like I'd seen a different film from the one I'd read about. I laughed at all the jokes – well there were a few that I didn't understand, but that could be to do with my age! The film is aimed at young people, there's no denying that. But my advice is – don't let that put you off. It's great.

5 *You hear a football coach talking about picking players for her team.*

Lots of students want to get onto the school football team and they just can't understand why they're not being picked. They show me fancy things they can do with the ball, bouncing it from knee to head and that sort of thing, and demonstrate good communication on the pitch – all of which is great of course. But if they get out of breath after 15 minutes, that's no good, and I see a lot of that. So that's the area I'm concentrating on at the moment, in my selections.

6 *You hear a student talking to his teacher about a picture for an art competition.*

Teacher: Your painting looks great, Greg! Do you think you can finish it by this evening? That's when you need to deliver it to the town hall for the judging, isn't it?

Greg: That's right – shouldn't be a problem. It's finished really, but I need to deal with this section here, where I accidentally painted over a really important figure. I'm not sure I can get it back to how it was. It's such a shame.

Teacher: Just take your time, it'll be fine. What are you going to call the painting?

Greg: I've got no idea to be honest. Something will come to me at the last minute, it usually does!

7 *You hear a girl talking about her new part-time job.*

I'm surprised how much I'm enjoying my new job to be honest. I have to get up really early, that's the only thing I don't like. But I've noticed that I'm getting fitter and stronger – it's all the manual work, I guess. I love being outdoors all day, even when it rains and I get all muddy. I have made a couple of mistakes. I pulled out some bushes one day that I thought were dead, but apparently they weren't. The home-owner wasn't too pleased about that!

8 *You hear a boy talking about a school trip.*

I've never been on a school trip like that one. We did so many different things – and actually often didn't really have enough time to get the most out of each one. I could have spent a lot longer at the beach to be honest, and a bit less time at the museum. But I'm not complaining. It was such a relief to get out of the classroom for a while and do something a bit different. Some of the kids were really tired at the end – I'm not sure everyone enjoyed it that much.

Acknowledgements

The authors and publishers acknowledge the following sources of copyright material and are grateful for the permissions granted. While every effort has been made, it has not always been possible to identify the sources of all the material used, or to trace all copyright holders. If any omissions are brought to our notice, we will be happy to include the appropriate acknowledgements on reprinting and in the next update to the digital edition, as applicable.

Screenshot

Screenshots taken from *Compact First for Schools Third Edition Workbook* by Joanna Kosta. Copyright © 2023 Cambridge University Press & Assessment.

Photography

Front cover photography by DisobeyArt/iStock/Getty Images Plus; Sir Francis Canker Photography/Moment; vladj55/iStock/Getty Images Plus; fitopardo.com/Moment; EnginKorkmaz/iStock Editorial/Getty Images Plus; Laurie Noble/DigitalVision; Pawel Toczynski/Photographer's Choice.

Typesetting

Typeset by Hyphen S.A.